Sugarfree
New Orleans©

A Cookbook based on the
Glycemic Index

Written by
Deanie Comeaux Bahan

for information, visit us at
www.toutsuite.com

ISBN 0-9660804-0-8
Library of Congress Catalog Card Number
LOC# 97-80696

First Printing   September, 1997
Second Printing   November, 1997
Third Printing   March, 1998
Fourth Printing   July, 1998
Fifth Printing   June, 1999

**Published by
AFM Publishing, L.L.C.
New Orleans, Louisiana**
www.toutsuite.com

Table of Contents

From Me to You:

I DON'T WANT TO BE FAT! No matter how many jokes I make about "passing up slim and going for voluptuous" or how many times I say, "big is beautiful," I don't want to be fat!

During my many years of agonizing over my size, I think I have tried every diet that has come along. They all worked – I lost ten pounds each time! But then I gained back that ten plus five or ten more as soon as I quit.

A regular diet yo-yo!

The books and programs all say, "This shouldn't be a diet, this should be a new way of life!" If you are at all like me, trying to tell yourself that a stalk of raw celery is a satisfying "new way of life" just doesn't work. Trying to tell yourself that a carrot stick can be as good as a bowl of ice cream is a delusion impossible to conjure. Weighing every bite that goes into your mouth can't be fun . . . but then neither is checking out the bulges in the mirror.

I've tried both over the counter and prescription diet pills. Redux did nothing and phen/fen made me climb the walls. Again, I lost the weight and then gained back more. A regular diet yo-yo! To make matters even worse, I live in New Orleans, one of the world's gastronomic capitals.

One day, a friend suggested trying **SugarBusters!**™1 What's one diet more or less going to hurt, I thought. And so, I bought the book. And I read it like most people do, skipping over the scientific parts, thinking that the Glycemic Index was not of great concern to me. But, I thought, this sounds like my kind of diet – steak, cheese, nuts, and ice cream.

5

I started on *Sugar Busters!* four months ago. I have lost twenty-six pounds since then and I still have more to lose. When I finish *Sugar Busters!* will I gain it back? This time I really don't think so because I don't think I will ever "finish" *Sugar Busters!* It may not be a whole new way of life, but it is a whole new way of eating and I think I will continue to eat this way forever. Why not? With a few simple modifications, I'm eating most of the foods I love and I'm on my way to being slim. I'm not hungry, I have more energy, and I feel great.

I had been on the diet for about a month and a half when something a great deal more important than my own new on-the-way-to-slim-and-trim figure happened. My husband, Mark, who is a non-diet-compliant diabetic heart patient was hospitalized. His blood sugar was 500+, his cholesterol was 400+, and his trig-lycerides were over 700. His doctors talked to him, the nutritionists talked to him, our children talked to him, and, as usual, he gave lip ser-vice to trying to go back to his low fat, low sugar diet. I knew that once again he would try for a week or two until his cravings for a good juicy steak, milk, and eggs got the better of him.

There was only one way to keep Mark on his diet...

He was in the hospital for ten days and, sitting at his bedside, I had lots of time to re-read my *Sugar Busters!* book. Suddenly, I realized that this book was written for him. If you take care of the sugar, it said, your body can handle the fat. Cut out the sugar, it said, and your cholesterol and tryglycerides will drop. It's worth a try, I said, so let's make a deal. I told him that if he could give up his sugary sodas and other sweets, he could keep his steak, milk, and eggs. He was skeptical but agreed to try. Four weeks later he went back to the hospital, but this time just for blood work. His blood sugar was 98; his cholesterol, 144; his tryglycerides, 72. It worked!

And so I became a rabid convert. I searched bookstores and libraries for more information on the Glycemic Index. Not finding much, I turned to the Internet. There I found more — over 400 links when I did a search on the term "Glycemic Index." By far the most helpful of these was Rick Mendosa's Web site at http://www.mendosa.com. Rick has the best all around GI information, links to a lot of other GI sites, and information on Professor Jennie Brand Miller's *The G.I. Factor*. He was also kind enough to answer a lot of my own questions by e-mail.

Recently, NBC's Dr. Bob Arnot published his wonderful new book **Dr. Bob Arnot's Revolutionary Weight Control Program** which is, in large part, also based on the Glycemic Index. He refers to the GI as the "*Glucose Load*", but the message is the same -- eat high fiber, add protein, curb the fat, and dump the sugars and refined carbos. It is published by Little Brown & Co. and is available at most book-stores. There are great reviews of it on the Internet.

The Glycemic Index

What is the Glycemic Response?
Your body's glycemic response is the rate at which your body converts foods to blood sugar. Foods that have a high glycemic response create a high level of blood sugar. This high blood sugar pro-duces a high level of insulin which helps process the sugar your body needs to do its work and then stores the excess as fat. A high level of insulin causes the sugar to be stored faster. This causes your energy level to drop and causes feelings of hunger and cravings for even more sugar.

Tons of GI studies...

How is the Glycemic Index measured?
Hundreds of GI studies have been done that rank selected foods to an in-dex. Confusingly, there are two different indexes that have been used. One ranks the foods on a scale where glucose=100 and the other ranks the foods where white bread=100. Generally the "white bread index" is used in the United States, but since the *Sugar Busters!* book uses the "sugar index", I'm going to give you both.

7

In researching the Glycemic Index, I have found a lot of variations depending on the study referenced. There really is no one verifiable index. The lists that I give here are a compilation of what exists, most of it provided by Rick Mendosa. You may find, and some studies did, that your own body's response to an individual food may vary from the index.

And now . . . the Glycemic Index:

	Bread based Index	Glucose based Index
Bread		
Bagel, white	103	72
Barley flour bread	95	67
Bread stuffing	106	74
Hamburger bun	87	61
Melba toast	100	70
Rye Kernel bread	92	64
Wheat bread, white	100	70
Wheat bread, high fiber	97	68
Whole wheat bread	105	74
Pita bread, white	82	57
Pita bread, stone ground	63	44
Mixed grain bread	69	48
Breakfast Cereal		
All-bran	60	42
Bran Chex	83	58
Cheerios	106	74
Cocopops	110	77
Corn Chex	118	83
Cornflakes	119	83
Cream of Wheat	100	70
Crispix	124	87

Golden Grahams	102	71
Grapenuts	96	67
Muesli	80	56
Nutri-grain	94	66
Puffed Wheat	105	74
Rice Chex	127	89
Rice Krispies	117	82
Shredded Wheat	99	69
Special K	77	54
Total	109	76

Grains

Barley	49	34
Buckwheat	78	55
Bulgur	68	48
Cornmeal	98	69
Rice, white	126	88
Rice, brown	79	55
Rice, instant boiled 1 minute	65	46
Rice, instant boiled 6 minutes	128	90
Rice, wild	81	57
Rice, Basmati brown	see notes	

Crackers

Breton Wheat	96	67
Rice Cakes	110	77
Stoned Wheat Thins	96	67

Dairy Foods

Regular Ice cream	87	61
No Sugar Added ice cream	see notes	
Milk, full fat	39	27
Milk, skim	46	32
Yogurt, low fat, fruit & sugar	47	33
Yogurt, low fat, Nutrasweet	20	14

Fruit (See Notes)

Apple	54	38
Apple juice	58	41
Apricots	44	31
Banana	77	54
Cherries	32	22
Fruit cocktail, canned	79	55
Grapefruit	36	25
Grapefruit juice	69	48
Grapes	66	46
Kiwi	75	53
Mango	80	56
Orange	63	44
Orange juice	74	52
Pawpaw	83	58
Peach	60	42
Peach, canned	67	47
Pear	53	37
Pear, canned	63	44
Pineapple	94	66
Plum	55	39
Raisins	91	64
Watermelon	103	72

Pasta (See notes)

White pasta	79	55
Whole grain pasta	57	40

Root Vegetables

Beets	91	64
Carrots	101	71
Parsnips	139	97
Potato, instant	118	83
Potato, baked	121	85
Potato, new	81	57

Potato, boiled and mashed	104	73
Potatoes, french fried	107	75
Rutabaga	103	72
Tapioca	100	70
Yam	73	51

Snacks

Jelly beans	114	80
Life Savers	100	70
Mars Bar	97	68
Muesli Bars	87	61
Popcorn	79	55
Corn chips	105	74
Peanuts	21	15
Pretzels	116	81

Sugars

Honey	104	73
Fructose (see notes)	32	22
Glucose	143	100
Maltose	150	105
Sucrose	92	64
Lactose	65	46

Vegetables

Baked beans, canned	69	48
Black beans	43	30
Black-eyed peas	59	41
Butter beans	44	31
Chick peas, Garbanzo beans	47	33
Chick peas, canned	60	42
Fava beans	113	79
Green peas	68	48
Green vegetables	<21	<15

Kidney beans	42	29
Kidney beans, canned	74	52
Lima beans, baby, frozen	46	32
Navy beans	54	38
Pinto beans	55	39
Pinto beans, canned	64	45
Pumpkin	107	75
Soya beans	25	18
Split peas, yellow, boiled	45	32
Sweet corn	78	55
Tomatoes	<21	<15

One of the foods with the lowest GI ranking is the Indian bean Chana Dal. It is similar to the Garbanzo and can be found through many health food stores.

Rice and Pasta Notes:
Rice can really be really confusing. On the white bread index it ranges from 54, an acceptable number, to an outrageous 132. What's the difference? A substance called amylose. Long grain is better than short grain; brown is better than white; and brown Basmati rice seems to be the best available in the U.S. If you can't find Basmati in your local grocery store, try a health food store or gourmet shop. How long you cook the rice also makes a difference. Instant rice cooked for six minutes had a GI of 121; the same rice cooked for one minute had a GI of 65!

Pasta seems to work the same way. The less you cook it, the better it is for you. The longer the spaghetti and the broader the noodle, the better it is. And, once again, stay away from the overly processed pasta. The best, by far, is the stone ground whole grain pasta.

Fruit Notes:
There seems to be a whole lot of dissension about when to eat fruit. The *Sugar Busters!* book seems to be very clear about its recommendation

The Big Fruit Debate...

that fruit should only be eaten one hour before or two hours after other foods. However, none of the other GI references that I read even mentioned it. I asked GI guru, Rick Mendosa, and he told me that he follows that guideline himself although his nutritionist says it's not necessary. Personally, I have been using fruit as a mid-morning or mid-afternoon snack.

Because of this confusion, I have not used liquid fructose to sweeten any desserts; however, I have included a good many fruit desserts. It's up to you to use them or not or when to use them. Remember, the whole point is to feel good and to lose weight if you need to. What works for you, works!

Miscellaneous Notes:

- LEARN TO READ THE LABELS!!! Initially, grocery shopping is going to take a long time as you stand in the aisles reading labels on cans and boxes. You are really going to be shocked at the amount of sugar you have been eating without realizing it. Skip products that contain high fructose corn syrup, cornstarch, maltodextrin, or any "-ose" products (maltose, dextrose, etc.). These are all different forms of sugar. Remember that the order of ingredients has to do with the amount of the ingredient in the product.

The labels are shocking!!!

- When you purée a vegetable, you raise its number on the Glycemic Index because you destroy some of its fiber. I realize that some of my soup recipes call for puréed veggies. Even puréed, these veggies are relatively low on the Index. But, the more "chunks" you leave, the better for you.

Don't get the idea that you can stuff yourself with low GI and high fat foods and still lose weight. A well balanced diet and normal sized servings are a must. Snacks during the day can actually be good for you because they keep your blood sugar from dropping too low. Try snacking on cheese or a handful of peanuts. I usually leave a jar of nuts in my car in case hunger pangs hit as I am driving past a "bad food" place.

- Another question concerning the Glycemic Index is what happens to the GI numbers when you combine foods. One study showed that when you put butter on a potato, the combined glycemic response is lower than that of the potato alone. Of course, not eating the potato at all is even better!

The choice really is yours!

My Disclaimer:

I am not a doctor. I am not a nutritionist. I like to eat and I know how to cook. I have read a lot about the Glycemic Index and I can tell you that there is still a lot of confusion out there. The recipes that I have included in this book are in accordance with most of the research. The best thing that I can tell you about these recipes is that they have worked for us and they taste great!

As with all diet and exercise programs, check with your own doctor before you begin.

Deanie Comeaux Bahan

Deanie Comeaux Bahan
New Orleans, Louisiana

Acknowledgements

Special thanks go to Leighton Steward, Dr. Morrison Bethea, Dr. Samuel Andrews, and Dr. Luis Balart, the authors of *Sugar Busters!* Their book has taught me how to eat right and it may just have saved my husband's life.

My parents, Dr. Clifford and Elisa Comeaux, taught us the importance of a close and caring family. The also taught us that good cooking can be a demonstration of love. Good food can nourish the soul as well as the body — good Creole and Cajun food that is!

My husband, Mark, and my son, Remy Gross for their love and support; my sisters, Neila Eckler and Ann Legleu for their recipes; my brother, Walter Comeaux, for his legal expertise; Simon Mexic for introducing me to *Sugar Busters!*; Rosalie Boudreaux for inspiration; Tina Kemp for her interest; and Donald Ray Lalanne, Evelyn Hyams, Howard and Mary Penton, and the rest of our family for their faith and support.

Thanks to Rick Mendosa, a Writer on the Web, for his advice; Alan Watts and Jim Stone of Barclay Advestments and Nancy Watts and Marr Snyder of Tout Suite for all of their help in "getting it together."

**To my family
with love and gratitude**

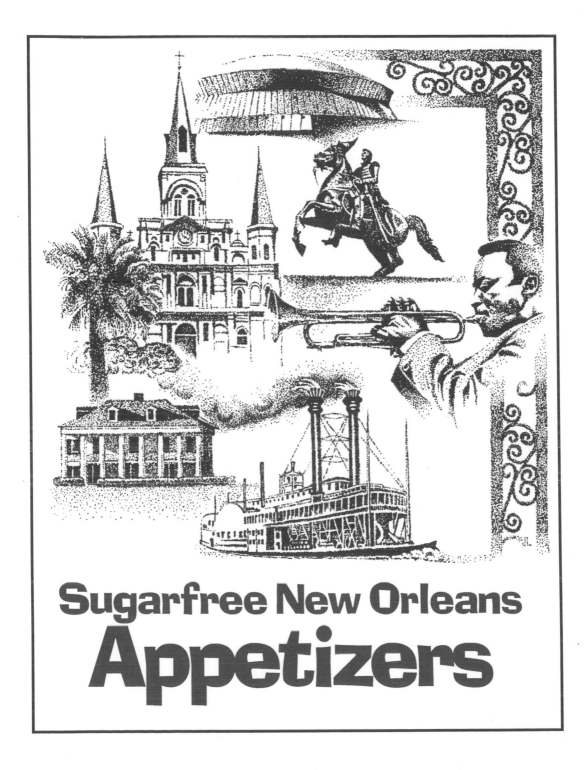

Sugarfree New Orleans
Appetizers

Caviar Deviled Eggs

6 hard boiled eggs
2 1/2 teaspoons lemon juice
3 tablespoons light sour
    cream
1/2 teaspoon salt
1/2 teaspoon pepper
1 jar caviar

Drain caviar in a very fine sieve. Rinse with cold water and allow to drain dry.

Slice eggs in half lengthwise and remove yolks. Mash yolks with lemon juice, sour cream, salt, and pepper until fairly smooth. Spoon the yolk mixture into the egg white halves making a small "dent" in the center of each. Fill each hollow with caviar.

If you have time and want to show off a little, pipe the yellow into the egg white with a pastry bag and tip and then fill with the caviar.

Baked Brie and Artichokes

1 small round Brie cheese
1/3 cup artichoke hearts,
    drained and chopped
1/2 teaspoon minced garlic
1/4 teaspoon chopped basil
1 teaspoon olive oil
salt and cayenne to taste

With a sharp knife, slice the Brie horizontally to form two rounds. Fit the bottom half into a greased round baking dish not much bigger than the Brie itself.

Mix the well drained (squeeze the excess liquid out) and finely chopped artichoke hearts with the garlic, basil, olive oil, salt and cayenne. Spread this mixture evenly on top of the Brie bottom. Put the top of the Brie back on. Bake this at 350F for about ten minutes or until the cheese is melted at the edges.

Feta and Blue Cheese Dip

1 cup light sour cream
2 ounces feta cheese
3 ounces light cream
    cheese
1/2 teaspoon sage
1/4 teaspoon basil
1/4 teaspoon thyme
1/2 teaspoon black pepper
1/2 teaspoon minced garlic
3 ounces crumbled blue
    cheese

In a food processor or by hand, beat sour cream, feta, and cream cheese until smooth. Add sage, basil, thyme, pepper, and garlic and beat until well blended. Add the crumbled blue cheese and stir gently. Refrigerate this for several hours before using.

It's great with raw cauliflower, broccoli, celery, etc. Remember, no carrots! They are near the top of the Glycemic Index.

Dilly Dip

1/2 cup sugarless
    mayonnaise
1/2 cup sour cream
2 tablespoons chopped
    green onions
2 tablespoons chopped
    parsley
2 tablespoons fresh dill
1/2 teaspoon lemon juice
1/2 teaspoon salt
1/4 teaspoon pepper

Combine all ingredients in a bowl. Stir until well mixed. This can be made ahead and then covered and refrigerated for up to 3 days.

Serve with broccoli or fresh asparagus.

Curried Crab Spread

8 ounces cream cheese,
    softened
1/4 cup sour cream
1 teaspoon lemon juice
1/2 teaspoon crushed garlic
1 teaspoon curry powder
6 ounces crab meat

Mix all ingredients except crab meat until well blended. Fold in crab meat gently. Serve with stone ground, no-sugar-added crackers.

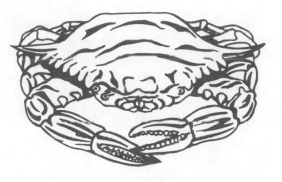

Guacamole

1 large avocado, ripened
1 tablespoon minced onion
1 jalapeno pepper, seeded
    and diced
1 teaspoon lime juice
1 teaspoon lemon juice
1/2 teaspoon ground cumin
1 small peeled tomato –
    seeded and diced
Salt and pepper to taste

Slice avocado, remove pit, and peel. To keep the avocado from darkening, submerge it in cold water and then drain.

In a bowl, mash the avocado with a fork leaving small chunks. Stir in the onion, the finely diced jalapeno, lime juice, lemon juice, cumin, salt, pepper, and tomato. Cover well and refrigerate. Serve chilled as an appetizer with stone ground crackers or on lettuce leaves as a salad.

Lacy Cheese

1/2 pound Monterey jack cheese

Preheat oven to 350F. Cut cheese into cubes that are about 1/2" square. Place them on a lightly greased baking sheet leaving a generous two inch border between cubes. Bake about 6 minutes, watching carefully. Remove from the oven when the melted cheese is bubbly. Let the "lace" cool in the pan for several minutes. Remove with a spatula and allow to harden before storing. Chill for storing, but serve at room temperature.

You can sprinkle the lace lightly with garlic powder, paprika, or other spices immediately after removing from the oven.

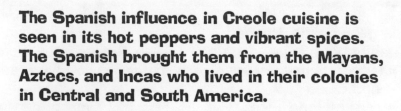

The Spanish influence in Creole cuisine is seen in its hot peppers and vibrant spices. The Spanish brought them from the Mayans, Aztecs, and Incas who lived in their colonies in Central and South America.

The Spanish had a great influence in New Orleans architecture also. Thanks to the enclosed patios and graceful wrought iron, the French Quarter looks far more Spanish than French!

Mushrooms Italiano

1½ pounds fresh mush-
    rooms
3/4 pound Italian sausage
1 tablespoon olive oil
1 package frozen spinach,
    thawed and drained
1/4 teaspoon salt
1/2 pound cheddar cheese
1/2 cup ricotta cheese
1/4 cup olive oil

Clean mushrooms, removing stems. Pat dry and set aside.

Remove casing from sausage and crumble into a frying pan. Cook thoroughly, about 8 minutes. Remove sausage from pan and drain well. Put the sausage into a large bowl. Pour all of the drippings out of the pan. Add olive oil to pan and sauté dried spinach for about a minute, adding the salt. Add the spinach to the sausage. Stir in cheddar and ricotta, mixing well.

Coat the mushrooms by tossing in the olive oil. Stuff the mushrooms with the sausage mixture and bake for fifteen minutes.

Piquant Pecans

1 pound pecan halves
6 tablespoons butter
2 tablespoons soy sauce
2 teaspoons salt
1/2 teaspoon black or
    red pepper
1/2 teaspoon garlic powder

Melt butter in a large baking pan. Toss pecans in the butter and soy sauce to coat. Bake for 8 minutes at 300F. While the pecans are baking, mix the salt, pepper, and garlic powder. Remove the nuts from the oven, sprinkle with the seasoning mix and toss. Serve warm or at room temperature. Store in an airtight container.

New Orleans Red Bean Dip

1 cans red kidney beans
4 tablespoons olive oil
2 tablespoons lemon juice
1 teaspoon minced garlic
Salt and pepper to taste
Tabasco sauce to taste
Red bean liquid

Drain the red beans, reserving the liquid. In a food processor or blender, mix the drained beans and the olive oil. Add the lemon juice, garlic, salt, pepper, and Tabasco and whirl a little longer.

If the mixture needs to be thinned a little to be used for a dip, add a little of the red bean liquid that you saved. You don't want the dip to be too thin, though. It should be able to hold its own shape.

Pickled Okra

3 pounds small okra pods
2 teaspoons dill seed
1 large onion, sliced thin
2 teaspoons celery seed
3 teaspoons minced garlic
3 jalapeno chile peppers
2 cups vinegar
4 cups water
1/3 cup salt

Sterilize jars in boiling water. Wash the okra and pat dry. Divide the cleaned whole okra, dill seed, onion, celery seed, and garlic between the jars and put one pepper in each.

In a pot, bring the vinegar, water, and salt to boil. Carefully ladle this brine over the okra in each jar. Cap each jar immediately. Allow to marinate unrefrigerated for at least a week before using.

Simple Cold Crab Dip

1 cup crabmeat
1/3 cup blue cheese
1/2 cup light cream cheese
1 tablespoon lemon juice
2 tablespoon sugarfree
. mayonnaise
1/2 tablespoon Worcester-
shire sauce

Let cheeses soften and then blend well with the lemon juice, mayonnaise, and Worcestershire sauce. Fold the crabmeat in gently.

Pita Scoops

1 package pita bread, stone
ground whole grain
olive oil
Minced garlic (optional)
Salt and pepper (optional)

Since corn chips, potato chips, etc. are near the top of the Glycemic Index, it's sometimes hard to find something to serve with the low GI dips. There are several no sugar added stone ground crackers available. In addition to these, you can make your own Pita Scoops.

Preheat oven to 400F. Cut pita bread edges carefully so you can split them into rounds. Brush each round with garlic soaked olive oil. Sprinkle with salt and pepper if you want to.

Stack the pita bread and cut into wedges. Place the wedges in a single layer on a baking sheet and bake about five minutes or until the wedges are crisp. Store in an airtight container.

Smoked Oyster Ball

8 ounces softened light
    cream cheese
1 tablespoon sugarless
    mayonnaise
1 teaspoon lemon juice
1/4 teaspoon minced garlic
Salt and pepper to taste
1/4 cup chopped ripe olives
1 can smoked oysters,
    drained and chopped
paprika

In a bowl combine the cream cheese, mayonnaise, lemon juice, minced garlic, salt and pepper. Blend well. Blend in chopped olives and oysters. Chill until the mixture becomes firm. Form into a ball or log and sprinkle with paprika.

Spinach Dip

1 package frozen chopped
    spinach
1 cup sugarfree mayon-
    naise
1 cup light sour cream
1/2 cup green onion,
    chopped fine
1/2 cup chopped parsley
1 tablespoon lemon juice
1 teaspoon dill
Salt and pepper to taste

Thaw and drain the spinach, squeezing all of the liquid out. In a bowl, combine all of the other ingredients. Add the spinach and mix until well blended.

Serve chilled with bite sized raw veggies (no carrots!!!) or stone ground crackers.

Sweet Potato Chips

4 large sweet potatoes
Peanut oil
Salt to taste

Hard to believe, but sweet potatoes are much, much lower on the Glycemic Index than white potatoes!

You will probably need a meat slicer or the slicing attachment on a food processor to slice the sweet potatoes thin enough. They should be cut between 1/16" and 1/8" thick.

Wash the potatoes and pat dry. Slice as described above. Pat the slices dry. Heat about two inches of oil to 300F on a cooking thermometer. Fry potatoes, a few at a time, for about 3 minutes or until lightly browned. Turn the potatoes while they are frying. Remove the chips from the oil with a slotted spoon and drain well on paper towels. Sprinkle with salt to taste. Store in an airtight container.

During the 1791 uprising in Haiti, several thousand people from Santo Domingo immigrated to New Orleans. They brought with them a great expertise in the preparation of seafood, one of the staples of Creole cuisine.

The great meeting place of these refugees was the Café des Exiles in the Vieux Carré. It later became the headquarters for the pirate Jean Lafitte and known as Lafitte's Blacksmith Shop.

Veggie Pickles

Selected vegetable
   -- *see note below*
2 cups vinegar
3/4 cup water
1 tablespoon salt
1/2 tablespoon cayenne
   pepper
1/2 teaspoon minced garlic
1 medium onion, sliced thin
4 fresh dill weeds
4 packets sugar substitute

In a large pot, combine the vinegar, water, salt, cayenne, and garlic. Bring to a boil and then simmer for 15 minutes. Add the cleaned vegetable and the onion slices and cook for three more minutes. Remove from heat and stir in the sugar substitute. Using tongs or a slotted spoon, put the vegetables in sterilized jars and pour the pickling juices in. Put dill weed in each jar, seal, and refrigerate when cool.

Note: All of the following vegetables work well; you might want to try a combination: green beans, celery, cauliflower, cucumbers, and broccoli.

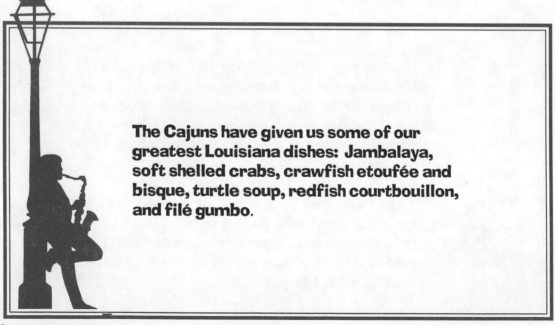

The Cajuns have given us some of our greatest Louisiana dishes: Jambalaya, soft shelled crabs, crawfish etoufée and bisque, turtle soup, redfish courtbouillon, and filé gumbo.

Greek Garbanzo Spread

1 can garbanzo beans
2 tablespoons olive oil
1/2 cup finely chopped
onions
1/2 cup finely chopped
green onions
1/3 cup finely chopped
parsley
1 1/2 teaspoon minced
garlic
2 tablespoons toasted
sesame seeds
2 tablespoons lemon juice
1/2 teaspoon oregano
salt and pepper to taste
Tabasco sauce to taste

In a food processor, blender, or grinder, mash the garbanzo beans and then remove them to a bowl.

In a skillet, sauté the onions, green onions, parsley, and garlic until tender. Add this mixture to the beans and blend well. Add the sesame seeds, lemon juice, oregano, salt, pepper, and Tabasco.

Refrigerate before serving.

Dill Sauce

1 pint light sour cream
1/4 cup minced onion
1/4 cup minced green onion
1/4 teaspoon celery seed
1/4 teaspoon garlic powder
2 tablespoons fresh dill

Mix all of the ingredients together until they are well blended and then chill.

This sauce is good with fresh asparagus and with boiled shrimp.

Artichoke Quiche Squares

**2 jars marinated artichoke
      hearts**
1/4 cup minced onion
1 clove garlic, minced
1/4 teaspoon oregano
**2 tablespoons parsley,
      chopped fine**
4 eggs
**1/4 cup crushed stone
      ground crackers**
1/4 teaspoon salt
1/4 teaspoon black pepper
Tabasco sauce to taste
**2 cups grated Cheddar
      cheese**

Drain the artichoke hearts reserving liquid. Chop the artichokes very fine and set them aside.

In a small saucepan cook the onions, garlic, oregano, and parsley in about half of the reserved marinade over medium heat for 5 minutes. Remove from heat and set aside.

In a bowl, beat all of the eggs until blended. Add chopped artichokes, cracker crumbs, salt, pepper, and Tabasco and mix well. Stir in the cheddar cheese and the cooked marinade mixture. Pour into a greased 9x9 inch baking pan. Bake at 325F (300F if using a glass pan) for 35 to 40 minutes or until firm.

Cut into large squares to serve as a vegetable for dinner or into small squares to use as appetizers. This dish freezes well.

Cream Cheese and Herbs

16 oz. light cream cheese,
   softened
1 tablespoon minced green
   onion
1 clove garlic, minced
1/2 teaspoon lemon juice
1/2 teaspoon dill
1/2 teaspoon basil
1/2 teaspoon thyme
1/2 teaspoon tarragon
Salt and pepper to taste

Combine all ingredients and chill. This is best made several hours or even a day ahead of serving.

Artichoke Spread

1 can artichoke hearts
1 jar black or red caviar
1 cup light sour cream
8 ounces light cream
   cheese
1/2 teaspoon salt
Tabasco sauce to taste

Drain the artichoke hearts and squeeze out as much liquid as possible. Pat dry. Dice the artichokes finely and set aside.

Drain the caviar in a very fine sieve and run under water to remove the black liquid. Allow to drain well.

In a bowl, mix the sour cream and cream cheese until well blended. Add artichoke hearts, salt and Tabasco and mix. Fold caviar in carefully. Cover and refrigerate. Serve chilled.

Baked Artichoke Squares

2 tablespoons chopped
    onion
1 teaspoon crushed garlic
a little olive oil
3 egg whites
1 whole egg
1/4 cup crushed stone
    ground crackers
3 tablespoons parsley,
    chopped fine
1/4 teaspoon dried dill
1/8 teaspoon cayenne
    pepper
1 cup low-fat mozzarella
    cheese, grated
1/2 cup low-fat ricotta
    cheese
10 oz. marinated artichoke
    hearts, drained and
    chopped

Preheat oven to 350F. Lightly oil an 8-inch square baking pan. In a heavy skillet over medium-high heat, sauté onion and garlic in olive oil until soft but not browned. Beat the egg whites until soft peaks form. In a bowl mix the whole egg, cracker crumbs, parsley, dill, cayenne, cheeses, and artichokes. Add sautéed onion and garlic and fold in the egg whites.

Pour into greased baking pan. Bake until set - about 30 minutes. Let cool, then cut into squares. Serve warm or cold.

New Orleans really is a large melting pot. There are now more people in New Orleans of Italian descent than there are French. It's from them that we get our stuffed artichokes and love of olive oil.

We also have a large contingency of Yugoslavians. They are the ones who have developed our oyster industry. Without them there would be no Oysters Rockefeller, Bienville, or Foch!

Blue Cheese Ball

2 packages cream cheese,
    softened
8 ounces blue cheese,
    softened
2 tablespoons grated onion
1 teaspoon Worcestershire
    sauce
1/2 teaspoon Tabasco
    sauce
1/2 cup minced parsley
1/2 cup minced green
    onions
3/4 cup pecans or almonds
    finely chopped
paprika

In a food processor, combine the cream cheese, blue cheese, onion, Worcestershire sauce, and Tabasco. Blend well. Stir in parsley, green onions, and nuts.

Shape the mixture into a ball, wrap and refrigerate. Serve at room temperature after sprinkling with paprika. Serve with no-sugar-added stone ground crackers.

You might try shaping the ball like an apple and coating thoroughly with paprika. Stick a small, clean twig with several leaves in the top.

Brie and Salmon

1 round Brie cheese
1/2 pound smoked salmon,
    sliced very thin
1 small purple onion,
    sliced very thin
3 sprigs fresh dill
1 tablespoon capers

With a very sharp carving knife, slice the Brie horizontally in half forming two circles. Lay the thin sliced salmon and then the onions over the bottom half. Put the top half of the Brie back on forming a "sandwich." Lay the dill and capers on top decoratively.

Served this chilled, surrounded by stone ground crackers. This is an elegant dish that will definitely provoke "oohs and aahs!"

Blue Cheese Mushrooms

2 slices bacon
1 pound fresh mushrooms
3 tablespoons olive oil
1 tablespoon green onion,
    chopped fine
1 cup blue cheese,
    crumbled
4 ounces cream cheese,
    softened
1 teaspoon lemon juice

Cook bacon, draining well to remove as much grease as possible. Crumble and set aside. Clean mushrooms and pat dry. Remove mushroom stems and trim if necessary. Chop stems to small pieces.

In a skillet, cook mushroom stems and green onions in one teaspoon of the olive oil on medium heat for about 3-4 minutes. Pour this mixture into a bowl with the bacon, blue cheese, cream cheese, and lemon juice. Stir the mixture until it is totally blended.

Put the remaining two tablespoons of olive oil in your now empty skillet. Add the mushroom caps and stir them around to coat them with the olive oil. Do not cook the mushrooms very long.

Fill the mushrooms with the blue cheese mixture and arrange on a greased baking sheet. If you are not ready to serve the mushrooms yet, you can cover and refrigerate them at this point. Bake at 375F for 12 minutes or until the mushrooms are tender and the cheese is bubbly.

This can be served as an appetizer, but would also be really good as an accompaniment to a lean steak.

Easy Avocado Dip

1 ripe avocado
6 oz. light cream cheese
1 teaspoon sugarfree
    mayonnaise
1 tablespoon lemon juice
1/4 cup onion, coarsely
    chopped
1/8 teaspoon garlic powder
Salt and pepper to taste
Tabasco sauce to taste
Worcestershire sauce to
    taste

Peel the avocado and cut it into chunks, removing the pit. Put it into a food processor or blender with the cream cheese, mayonnaise, lemon juice, onion, garlic, salt, pepper, Tabasco, and Worcestershire sauce. Blend until smooth. You may want to add a drop of green food coloring for appearance

Shrimp Spread San Marco

1 pound boiled shrimp
1 package light cream
    cheese, softened
1/4 cup light sour cream
1 bunch green onions,
    chopped fine
1 tablespoon chopped
    parsley
1 tablespoon lemon juice
1 teaspoon Worcestershire
    sauce
Tabasco sauce to taste
Salt and pepper to taste

Peel shrimp and chop. Set aside. In a bowl, combine the cream cheese, sour cream, green onions, parsley, lemon juice, and Worcestershire sauce. Mix well to blend. Add the shrimp and season to taste.

Crab Jalapeno Dip

1 pound crabmeat, picked
   for shells
1/3 cup olive oil
1/2 cup evaporated skim
   milk
1 roll jalapeno cheese
8 ounces cheddar cheese
1/2 tablespoon Worcester-
   shire sauce
salt and pepper to taste

In a saucepan, put the crabmeat and the olive oil. Sauté for a few minutes. Add the milk and heat. Add the cheese and cook on low heat until melted. Add Worcestershire sauce, salt, and pepper. Serve warm.

Swedish Meat Balls

1/2 pound lean ground meat
1/4 teaspoon celery salt
1/2 teaspoon dry mustard
2 tablespoons sugar free
   mayonnaise
2 tablespoons finely
   crushed stone ground
   crackers
1/2 teaspoon onion salt
dash of curry powder
salt and pepper to taste
Tabasco sauce to taste

Mix all ingredients together, blending well. Shape into bite sized balls and broil until brown, turning once. These freeze well and can be reheated for fifteen minutes in a 350F oven. Serve hot with toothpicks.

These are good without any sauce, but if you want one, check the index of this book for the Island Barbeque Sauce.

Note: *I've looked really hard and still cannot find a commercially prepared barbeque sauce that is not loaded with sugar.*

Salsa Verde

1 tablespoon olive oil
1/2 cup onion, chopped
    fine
2 tablespoons stone ground
    whole grain flour
16 ounces canned tomatoes
    with juice, coarsely
    chopped
1 can green chiles, diced
1 clove garlic
¼ teaspoon ground cumin
salt and pepper to taste

In a sauce pan, cook the chopped onion in the olive oil on medium heat until the onion softens. Do not brown the onion. Stir flour into the oil, blending well. Stir in chopped tomatoes with juice, the chiles, garlic, cumin, salt, and pepper. Bring the mixture to a boil then simmer for 20 minutes until sauce is thickened, stirring occasionally. Chill before serving.

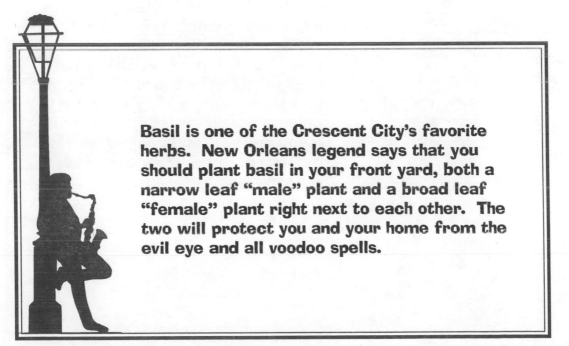

Basil is one of the Crescent City's favorite herbs. New Orleans legend says that you should plant basil in your front yard, both a narrow leaf "male" plant and a broad leaf "female" plant right next to each other. The two will protect you and your home from the evil eye and all voodoo spells.

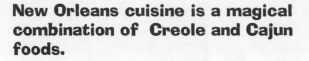

New Orleans cuisine is a magical combination of Creole and Cajun foods.

The Creoles were European highborn and Louisiana bred. Both their cooking and culture were greatly influenced by the French, Spanish, Africans, Italians, and even Germans who had settled in the area.

The word "Cajun" is a corruption of the word "Acadian." These were the French peoples exiled from Acadia in Nova Scotia, Canada. Upon exile, they made their way to the bayous of South Louisiana where they created a cuisine based on indigenous wild game and seafood cooked with local herbs and peppers and a French flair.

Sugarfree New Orleans
Salads

Bermuda Salad

1 head lettuce
1 head cauliflower
2 Bermuda onions, sliced
    thin
1/2 cup stuffed olives,
    sliced
1/2 cup Roquefort cheese,
    crumbled
1 egg
2 cups olive oil
4 packets sugar substitute
1 1/2 teaspoons salt
1 teaspoon dry mustard
1/2 teaspoon black pepper
1 tablespoon paprika
6 1/2 tablespoons vinegar

Clean the lettuce and cauliflower and break into salad sized bites. Put the lettuce, cauliflower, onion, olives, and crumbled cheese into a large salad bowl. Set aside.

In a blender, beat the egg and pour in the olive oil in a slow stream while whirling. Add the sweetener, salt, dry mustard, pepper, paprika, and vinegar. Whirl until well blended.

Pour the dressing over the salad, toss, and serve. If you have extra dressing, refrigerate it to use later.

Caesar Salad

1/2 cup olive oil
1/4 cup red wine vinegar
2 large garlic cloves, cut in
    quarters
2 tablespoons Worcester-
    shire sauce
1/4 teaspoon salt
1/4 teaspoon pepper
1/2 cup grated fresh
    Parmesan cheese
1 head romaine lettuce,
    torn in bite sizes
1 egg, beaten

Put the olive oil, vinegar, garlic, Worcestershire sauce, salt and pepper, and Parmesan in a jar and shake to mix. Refrigerate overnight.

Rinse the romaine and drain well. Pat dry with paper toweling. Add the beaten egg to the dressing and shake well. Pour over the romaine and serve.

41

Cole Slaw I

1 head green cabbage,
   cleaned and shredded
1 head purple cabbage,
   cleaned and shredded
1 cup mayonnaise, no sugar
   added
1/3 cup onion, chopped fine
1/4 cup lowfat milk
salt and pepper to taste

Mix mayonnaise, onion, and milk. Pour over shredded cabbage and season to taste. If you like a sweeter taste to your cole slaw, you can add a little artificial sweetener. Refrigerate and serve cold.

Cole Slaw II

1 head cabbage, shredded
1/4 cup parsley, shredded
1 medium onion
2 tablespoons olive oil
3 tablespoons vinegar
4 packets sugar substitute
1/4 teaspoon garlic powder
salt and pepper to taste

Put shredded cabbage and parsley in a salad bowl. Slice the onion thin and then cut the slice so that the strips are around 1" long. Add the onion to the cabbage. Mix the olive oil, vinegar, sweetener, and garlic powder well, pour over the cabbage mixture, and toss. Season with salt and pepper to taste.

Cucumbers in Sour Cream

1/2 teaspoon salt
1/2 teaspoon sugar
   substitute
1/2 teaspoon red pepper
1/3 cup vinegar
2/3 cup light sour cream
1 teaspoon chives
1/2 teaspoon paprika
3 cucumbers

Mix salt, sweetener, pepper, vinegar, sour cream, and chives well. Peel or score cucumbers and slice. Toss with dressing and sprinkle with paprika. Refrigerate and serve chilled.

Easy Tomato Aspic

2 cans stewed tomatoes, no
    sugar added
2 packages sugar free
    lemon jello
1 teaspoon salt
2 tablespoons vinegar

Put tomatoes in a saucepan and bring to a boil. Add the lemon jello, salt, and vinegar and stir until the jello is dissolved. Pour the mixture into tall, straight-sided drinking glasses and chill until firm. Unmold carefully - you may have to dip them in hot water for a minute - and slice.

If you like it that way, you can top the slices with a dollop of sugar free mayonnaise.

Greek Spinach Salad

2 bunches spinach
1/2 cup red onion, thinly
    sliced
1/2 cup cucumbers, thinly
    sliced
1/2 cup radishes, sliced
1/4 cup pine nuts or walnuts
1/4 cup Greek olives
4 ounces Feta cheese,
    crumbled
1 teaspoon Dijon mustard
1/2 tablespoon parsley
    chopped
1 green onion, sliced
1 tablespoon lemon juice
1 teaspoon minced garlic
2 tablespoons olive oil

Wash the spinach, removing the stems. Dry and tear into bite-size pieces. Toss spinach in a serving bowl with red onion, cucumbers, radishes, pine nuts, Greek olives, and half of the Feta.

In a blender mix remaining Feta, mustard, parsley, green onion, lemon juice, garlic, and olive oil. Pour over salad, toss, and serve.

Green Goddess Dressing

1 teaspoon minced garlic
2 tablespoons anchovies,
    chopped
3 tablespoons green onions
    chopped
1 tablespoon lemon juice
3 tablespoons tarragon
    vinegar
1/2 cup light sour cream
1/2 cup no-sugar-added
    mayonnaise,
1/4 cup chopped parsley
salt and pepper to taste

Mix all ingredients well and chill. This is best when made the day before you use it so that the flavors have time to blend. Serve over mixed salad greens.

Marinated Shrimp Salad

1 1/2 pounds large boiled
    shrimp,
1/2 cup tarragon vinegar
1/4 cup Creole or Dijon
    mustard
1/4 cup chopped parsley
2 tablespoons minced
    onion
1/4 cup chopped green
    onions
1 teaspoon minced garlic
2 teaspoons salt
1 teaspoon pepper
Tabasco to taste
1/2 cup olive oil
1 head lettuce

In a bowl, combine vinegar, mustard, parsley, onions, garlic, salt, pepper, Tabasco, and olive oil. Stir until well blended. Add shrimp and stir well. Cover and allow to marinate in the refrigerator all day or overnight.

Wash and drain lettuce. Pat dry. Cut or tear into shreds into a salad serving bowl. Use a slotted spoon to remove the shrimp from the marinade and add them to the lettuce. Use several spoons of the marinade as dressing. Add it to the salad and toss. Serve chilled.

Pickled Green Beans

2 pounds tender fresh
   green beans
3 cups vinegar
2 cups water
2 tablespoons mustard
   seeds
2 teaspoons peppercorns
2 teaspoons salt
1 cinnamon stick
1 1/2 teaspoons minced
   garlic
10 packets sugar substitute
   or to taste

Snap the ends off of the green beans and rinse well. Cook in boiling water for five minutes and then drain. In a pot, boil the vinegar, water, mustard seeds, peppercorns, salt, cinnamon, and garlic for ten minutes. Remove from heat. Remove the cinnamon stick and add the sugar substitute, stirring well. Pack the green beans loosely in sterilized, hot jars. Carefully pour the hot pickling liquid over the beans and seal the jars.

Roquefort Cheese Dressing

2 tablespoons mayonnaise,
   no-sugar-added
2 tablespoons lowfat milk,
   or buttermilk
3 tablespoons Roquefort
   cheese, crumbled
3 tablespoons olive oil
1 tablespoon tarragon
   vinegar
salt and pepper to taste

Add milk and cheese to mayonnaise and mix well. Add all other ingredients and stir well.

Great on salad or as a dip for raw vegetables.

Shrimp Salad

1 pound shrimp, boiled,
  peeled, coarsely
  chopped
2 tablespoons chopped
  green onion
2 stalks celery, chopped
1 tablespoon capers
2 hard-boiled eggs,
  chopped
2 1/2 tablespoons no-sugar-
  added mayonnaise
salt and pepper to taste

Mix all ingredients and chill. Shrimp salad is a great luncheon dish and can be served on lettuce leaves, with avocado, or inside of a scooped out tomato.

This recipe also works well using chicken or turkey instead of shrimp.

Sweet and Sauer Kraut

1 large can of sauerkraut,
  drained
1 cup finely chopped onion
1/2 cup finely chopped bell
  pepper
5 packets sugar substitute
1 cup finely chopped celery
1/4 cup vinegar

Combine all ingredients in a glass bowl or jar. Stir well and cover. Refrigerate overnight before serving. This can be kept in the refrigerator for several weeks.

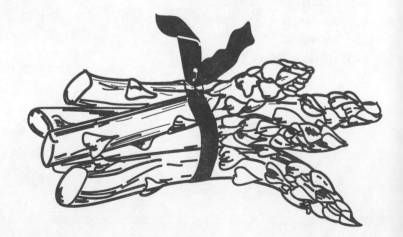

Cole Slaw Vinaigrette

1 head cabbage, shredded
1/3 cup chopped bell
    pepper
3 packets sugar substitute
1 teaspoon celery salt
1 teaspoon grated onion
3 tablespoons olive oil
1/3 cup vinegar
1 teaspoon dry mustard
salt and pepper to taste

Mix the bell pepper, sugar substitute, celery salt, grated onion, olive oil, vinegar, and dry mustard well to blend. Pour over the shredded cabbage and toss. Add salt and pepper to taste and toss again.

This sauce is also good on cucumbers.

Three Bean Salad

1 can red kidney beans
1 can green beans
1 can yellow beans
1 medium onion, sliced thin
3 packets sugar substitute
1/3 cup olive oil
2/3 cup vinegar
1 teaspoon salt
1/2 teaspoon pepper

Drain all of the beans and rinse the red ones. Put the beans and the sliced onions in a salad bowl. Sprinkle the beans and onions with the sweetener and toss to mix. Heat the olive oil, vinegar, salt, and pepper in the microwave or on top of the stove for several minutes. It is not necessary to bring it to a boil. Pour the hot liquid over the beans and toss. Cover and refrigerate for at least 24 hours. Serve chilled over shredded lettuce.

Antipasto Salad d'Arsena

lettuce, torn into bite sized
    pieces
onion, sliced thin
black olives, whole pitted
green olives, whole pitted
pimento, sliced
artichoke hearts, drained
    and quartered
tomatoes, quartered
hard boiled eggs, quartered
lean proscuitto, sliced in
    strips
provolone or Swiss cheese,
    cut in strips

Dressing:
1/3 cup olive oil
3 tablespoons wine vinegar
1/4 tablespoon dry mustard
1/4 tablespoon oregano
salt and pepper to taste

Arrange all of the salad items artfully in a large bowl. Mix the dressing ingredients together and pour over the salad. Do not toss.

We get two very important seasonings from the Choctaw Indians who lived on the north shore of Lake Pontchartrain -- filé (pronounced fee-lay) and bay leaves. Filé, which is used to thicken gumbo after it has finished cooking, is a fine powder ground from the leaves of the sassafras tree. Bay leaves, which come from laurel, are essential to most Creole soups, stews, and bean dishes.

Shrimp and Avocado Salad

2 pounds medium boiled,
    peeled shrimp
1 lemon, thinly sliced
1 small red onion, sliced
    thin
3/4 cup sliced ripe olives
2 tablespoons red wine
    vinegar
1/2 cup olive oil
1/2 cup lemon juice
2 teaspoons minced garlic
1 1/2 tablespoons Dijon
    mustard
1/4 teaspoon cayenne
salt and pepper to taste
2 ripe avocados, peeled
    and sliced
2 tablespoons finely
    chopped parsley

In a bowl, combine the shrimp, lemon slices, onion, and olives. Pour in the vinegar, half of the olive oil, and half of the lemon juice. Mix well and marinate for several hours or overnight.

In a jar, combine the remaining olive oil and lemon juice, the garlic, mustard, cayenne, salt and pepper and shake well.

Just before serving time, peel and slice the avocado and add it to the shrimp bowl. Pour on the dressing, add the parsley and toss.

Lakeview Salad

Various salad greens –
    romaine, ice burg, etc.
1/3 cup olive oil
1/3 cup grated cheddar
    cheese
1/3 cup crumbled blue
    cheese
1 raw egg, beaten
juice of 1 lemon

Combine all ingredients in a large salad bowl and toss to mix.

Pontchartrain Pasta Salad

1 pound stone ground
   whole grain pasta
1 pound cooked shrimp,
   peeled
1/3 cup grated fresh Parmesan cheese
4 green onions, finely
   chopped
1/4 cup chopped red or
   green bell pepper
Dressing:
   1/4 cup tarragon vinegar
   2 tablespoons water
   1 tablespoon olive oil
   1 tablespoon basil
   1teaspoon Dijon mustard

Cook the pasta according to the package directions. Do not use any salt and do not overcook. Drain well.

In a large bowl, toss the shrimp, Parmesan, onions, and bell pepper with the dressing ingredients. Add the pasta, toss, and chill.

Remember, the less you cook pasta, the lower it is on the Glycemic Index.

St. Charles Avenue Chicken Salad

3 cups diced cooked
   chicken
4 hard boiled eggs,
   chopped
1/2 cup chopped celery
1/2 cup chopped green
   onion
1 tablespoon chopped
   parsley
1/8 teaspoon garlic powder
1/2 cup no-sugar-added
   mayonnaise
1 teaspoon creole mustard
1/2 cup chopped pecans
salt and pepper to taste
cayenne pepper to taste

Combine all of the ingredients and mix well. Serve on lettuce leaves or stuffed in tomatoes or avocados.

Pasta Phiddipides

1/2 pound small boiled
   shrimp, peeled
1/2 pound stone ground
   whole grain pasta
10 cherry tomatoes, halved
1/4 cup ripe olives, sliced
1/4 cup thin sliced onion
3 ounces Feta cheese,
   crumbled

Dressing:
1/2 teaspoon dill
1 teaspoon minced garlic
1/4 cup chopped red onion
3 tablespoons lemon juice
1/3 cup olive oil
salt and pepper to taste

First, make your dressing by combining all of the dressing ingredients in a blender and whirling until fairly smooth.

Toss the shrimp and onions with a little of the dressing and refrigerate for at least 3 hours. Overnight would be okay. Also refrigerate the unused dressing.

Cook pasta according to directions. Drain and toss with marinated shrimp and onions, tomatoes, olives, and Feta. Use as much of the remaining dressing as you need.

Salad Dressing Provençal

1/2 cup olive oil
1 teaspoon salt
1/2 teaspoon freshly ground
   pepper
1 teaspoon minced garlic
tarragon to taste
2 tablespoons minced
   parsley
2 green onions, minced
1 tablespoon wine vinegar

Combine all ingredients in a jar. Shake well and pour over chilled salad greens and "Glycemic-Index-allowable" raw vegetables.

Tomato Vinaigrette Dressing

1 tablespoon Dijon mustard
2 tablespoons wine vinegar
1/2 cup olive oil
1 large tomato, peeled and
     diced small
2 green onions, minced
2 tablespoons minced
     parsley
1 tablespoon capers
1 teaspoon dill

Put all of the ingredients into a jar and shake well. Refrigerate for a while and then shake before using.

Garlic Mayonnaise

4 crushed garlic cloves
2 egg yolks
1 cup olive oil
juice of 1/2 lemon
salt and pepper to taste

Combine garlic and egg yolks. Add the olive oil a drop or two at a time, beating continuously. Do this for the first several tablespoons of oil. Then, pour the rest in a steady stream while beating. Add the lemon juice, salt and pepper to taste. Refrigerate.

Cajun foods are often laced with a great deal of pepper. Remember, though, the pepper should complement the food, not overpower it!

What kinds of peppers are grown in Louisiana? Red and green tabascos, serranos, Anaheim chilis, Louisiana sports, Torridos, Bahamian reds, birds eyes, cayennes, jalapenos . . .

Could You Ask for Anything More?

3/4 cup olive oil
1/4 cup vinegar
1 ½ packets of sugar
    substitute
3/4 teaspoon salt
1/4 teaspoon paprika
1/4 teaspoon dry mustard
1/4 teaspoon pepper

Combine all of the ingredients in a jar and shake well. Refrigerate.

Variations:

_____

_____

_____

_____

_____

_____

_____

_____

_____

_____

_____

_____

Sugarfree New Orleans
Soups & Sauces

Minestrone Taranto

1/2 cup olive oil
1/2 teaspoon minced garlic
2 cups chopped onions
1 cup chopped celery
1 small can no-sugar-added
    tomato paste
5 cans beef broth
3 cups water
1 cup shredded cabbage
1/8 teaspoon ground sage
salt and pepper to taste
1 whole zucchini, sliced
1 package frozen green
    beans, chopped
1 can red kidney beans
1 cup stone ground whole
    grain pasta, uncooked
Parmesan cheese, grated

In a large soup pot, sauté garlic, onion and celery in olive oil until soft. Stir in tomato paste, broth, water, cabbage, sage, salt, and pepper. Bring to a boil. Lower heat, cover, and simmer slowly for one hour. Add the vegetables and pasta and cook for ten minutes or until the pasta is just tender. Do not overcook.

Serve the minestrone with a small bowl of freshly grated Parmesan cheese. Let each guest add it as they wish.

Onion Soup Montmartre

1 1/2 pounds yellow onions,
    sliced thin
3 tablespoons butter
1 tablespoon olive oil
1 teaspoon salt
1 tablespoon stone ground
    whole grain flour
4 cans of beef broth
1/2 cup white wine
salt and pepper to taste

Cook the onions slowly with the butter and oil in a heavy soup pot for 15 minutes or until the onions are tender and golden. Blend in the flour. Add the beef stock, wine and season to taste. Simmer partially covered for 30-40 minutes, skimming occasionally.

Bayou Bouillabaisse

2 tablespoons butter
2 tablespoons olive oil
1 cup chopped onion
1/2 cup chopped celery
1/2 teaspoon minced garlic
1/4 cup stone ground whole
    grain flour
4 cups clam juice
12 ounces canned tomatoes
1/2 cup white wine
1 tablespoon lemon juice
2 tablespoons chopped
    parsley
2 bay leaves
salt and cayenne pepper to
    taste
2 pounds fish fillets, cut in
    chunks
1 pint oysters with liquid
1/2 pound peeled shrimp
1 cup crabmeat

Melt butter with olive oil in a large soup pot. Sauté onions, celery, and garlic until tender. Blend in the flour and cook until light brown. Stir in the clam juice and the oyster liquid slowly. Add tomatoes, wine, lemon juice, herbs, and seasonings to taste. Simmer on low heat for 1 hour.

Add fish and cook for ten minutes. Add shrimp, oysters, and crabmeat; cook five more minutes. Serve hot.

Basic Vegetable Soup

1 small onion, chopped
2 celery stalks, chopped
1/4 cup chopped bell
    pepper
4 tablespoons olive oil
5 cans beef broth
1 cup no-sugar-added
    tomato juice
1 cup chopped green beans
1 cup chopped zucchini
1 cup chopped cabbage
salt and pepper to taste

In a large soup pot, sauté the onion, celery, and bell peppers in the olive oil until tender. Add the broth, tomato juice, green beans, zucchini, and cabbage. Cover and simmer for about 45 minutes or until all the vegetables are done. Add the salt and pepper.

Remove about two cups of the mixture and put into blender. Puree this mixture and then return it to pot with rest of soup.

Allow the soup to sit for an hour or two so that the flavors can meld.

Beef and Cabbage Soup

1 pound lean beef stew
    meat, cut in bite sized
    chunks
3 tablespoons olive oil
2 onions, cut in small
    chunks
3 celery stalks, chopped
3 cans beef broth
1 head cabbage, cut in
    small chunks
salt and pepper to taste

Trim meat of all fat and brown in the olive oil. Add onions and celery and sauté for several minutes. Add the beef broth, cover, and simmer for one and a half hours.

Add cabbage, salt, and pepper and simmer for another half hour.

Bucktown Navy Bean Soup

1 cup navy beans
2 celery stalks, chopped
1/2 onion, chopped
1/2 teaspoon minced garlic
1/2 pound lean ham chunks
salt and pepper to taste
3 tablespoons olive oil
3 tablespoons stone ground
    whole grain flour
Tabasco sauce to taste

Wash the beans and let them soak in water overnight.

In a large soup pot, put the drained beans and five cups of water, the celery, onion, garlic, ham, salt, and pepper. Bring to a boil and then simmer, covered, for three hours or until the beans are very tender.

Put about two cups of the soup (not the ham) into a blender with the olive oil and flour. Purée this mixture. Add the purée back to the soup pot and add Tabasco to taste. Simmer for another twenty minutes or until the soup is slightly thickened.

Quick Tomato Soup

2 teaspoons olive oil
1/2 cup chopped onion
2 pounds tomatoes, puréed
2 cups chicken broth
1/4 cup chopped fresh basil
1/2 teaspoon cayenne
    pepper
salt to taste
coarsely grated Parmesan
    cheese

In a soup pot, sauté onion in olive oil until tender. Add puréed tomatoes, broth, basil, pepper, and salt. Simmer for about ten minutes. Serve with Parmesan cheese.

Variations:

- **Creamy Tomato** – add 1/2 pint light cream

- **Curried Tomato** -- eliminate the cheese and add 2 1/4 teaspoons curry powder and 1/2 pint light cream

- **Tomato Vegetable** – add cooked, diced vegetables such as green beans, cabbage, or zucchini.

Vegetable Soup Supreme

1 onion, sliced
2 celery stalks, chopped
2 tablespoons olive oil
2 zucchini, sliced
3 tomatoes, cut in chunks
1 1/2 teaspoons salt
1/2 teaspoon pepper
1 can green beans
1 can red kidney beans
1/4 pound stone ground
    whole grain pasta
1/4 cup no-sugar-added
    tomato paste
1/4 cup grated fresh
    Parmesan cheese
3 garlic cloves
1/4 teaspoon salt
2 tablespoons basil
1 tablespoon olive oil

In a large soup pot, sauté the onion and celery in olive oil until tender. Add 4 cups of hot water, the zucchini, and tomatoes. Bring to a boil and then allow to simmer for about ten minutes.

Add salt, pepper, drained green and red beans, and pasta. Simmer for another ten minutes

In a blender, put the tomato paste, cheese, garlic, salt, basil, and olive oil. Process to a smooth paste and stir into soup. Serve hot.

Take the number of cooks in the world and multiply by ten. That is the approximate number of different types of gumbo that can be made. But to truly be gumbo they must have two things: first a roux, and then either filé or okra as a thickening agent.

Leftovers Soup

1 1/2 pounds leftover meat
1 quart water
1 bay leaf
1 cup chopped onions
2 teaspoons minced garlic
2 tablespoons olive oil
1 quart canned chicken or
    beef broth
1/2 cup barley
1 teaspoon thyme
1 teaspoon oregano
1 teaspoon marjoram or
    rosemary
any other "chopable"
    leftover vegetables
salt and pepper to taste

Cut all the meat off the bones and into bite-sized pieces. Set it aside. Put the bones and the bay leaf into the quart of water and bring to a boil. Boil, uncovered, for fifteen minutes. Remove bones from the stock.

In a soup pot, sauté the onion and garlic in the olive oil until tender. Add the stock, the canned broth, and the barley and simmer uncovered for ten minutes. Add the meat, the thyme, oregano, marjoram or rosemary, and veggies. Continue cooking for ten more minutes. Add salt and pepper to taste.

Note: If your leftover meat has no bones, use an additional quart of canned beef broth and eliminate the water.

Modified Canned Broth

32 ounces canned chicken
    broth
1 teaspoon dried thyme
2 turns fresh ground pepper
1 teaspoon minced garlic
1/2 cup finely chopped
    green onion

Mix all ingredients in a saucepan. Cover and simmer over medium heat for five minutes or until garlic and onion are soft.

Three Bean & Lentil Soup

1 large onion, chopped
2 teaspoons cumin seed
2 quarts chicken broth
1 cup dried lentils
4 cups water
16 ounces black beans,
    rinsed and drained
16 ounces garbanzo beans,
    rinsed and drained
16 ounces red kidney
    beans, rinsed and
    drained
1 pound tomatoes, puréed
1/2 cup fresh basil, chopped
1/2 cup fresh parsley,
    chopped
1/2 teaspoon red pepper
salt to taste
1 tablespoon fresh, parsley
    minced
1/2 cup light sour cream

In a large soup pot, simmer the onion and cumin seeds in the broth, covered, for five minutes. Add the water and lentils and cook for forty more minutes. Put a little of the soup liquid into the blender with a cup of mixed black beans and garbanzo beans and partially purée.

Add the purée and the remaining beans to the soup pot. Stir in the puréed tomatoes, basil, parsley, pepper, and salt. Simmer for another thirty minutes.

You can serve each bowl of soup with a dollop of sour cream and a sprinkle of parsley.

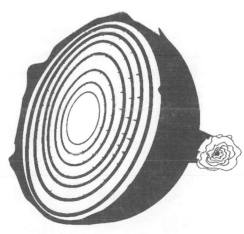

Puréed Vegetable Soup

4 cups raw vegetable***
1 large yellow onion, peeled
    and chopped
2 tablespoons olive oil
3 cans chicken broth
1 tablespoon lemon juice
1/2 cup light cream
1 teaspoon salt
1/4 teaspoon crushed red
pepper flakes
2 tablespoons minced fresh
    herb***

Note: Remember, when you purée a vegetable, you send it climbing up the Glycemic Index. Don't overdo it.

In a covered pot with 3/4 cup water, steam raw vegetable for about ten minutes or until soft. Put the vegetable with the water in a blender. Purée and set aside.

Put olive oil and chopped onion in large saucepan over medium heat and sauté until the onion is tender. Add it to the purée in the blender and process again.

Return the mixture to the soup pot and add the broth, lemon juice, cream, salt, red pepper, and herb. Simmer, stirring continuously, until the soup has thickened slightly and all the flavors have blended, about 10 minutes.

Variations for the vegetables and herbs:

- Broccoli and minced garlic.

- Cauliflower and minced garlic; or curry

- Cucumber and savory (substitute plain lowfat yogurt for cream in soup and serve chilled)

- Green bean and thyme.

- Spinach and nutmeg.

Oyster & Artichoke Bisque

3 dozen oysters, save liquid
3 cans artichoke hearts,
   drained & chopped fine
1/2 stick butter
1/4 cup olive oil
1/4 cup green onion,
   chopped fine
2 cloves garlic, chopped
   fine
1/4 cup parsley, chopped
   fine
3/4 cup stone ground whole
   grain flour
2 cans chicken broth
2 teaspoons thyme
2 bay leaves
salt and pepper to taste
2 cups lowfat evaporated
   milk
1/2 cup light sour cream

Drain oysters, saving the liquid. Be sure all shells are removed. Chop oysters and cook 10 minutes in the liquid. Set aside.

In a heavy soup pot, melt the butter with the olive oil. Sauté half of the green onions, all of the garlic and parsley for 5 minutes. Blend in flour carefully and cook for 5 minutes stirring constantly. Add chicken stock. Cook until the mixture begins to thicken. Add thyme, bay leaves, salt & pepper. Stir in artichokes and oysters. Bring to a boil and add milk and sour cream. Simmer at low heat for 15 minutes. Top with remaining green onions when serving.

Black Bay Oyster Soup

3 dozen oysters
3 cups milk, lowfat
3/4 cup light cream
2 tablespoons butter
salt and pepper to taste
1 tablespoon minced fresh
    parsley
1 tablespoon minced green
    onion

Go through the oysters with clean hands to make sure there are no shell pieces. Put the oysters with their liquid into a pot and cook until the oyster edges start to curl. Drain the oysters, reserving the liquid.

In the microwave or, carefully, on top of the stove, bring the milk and cream just to the boiling point. Put the butter in the pot with the oysters and add the scalded milk and cream. Add salt and pepper to taste. Serve hot but do not boil. Sprinkle the parsley and green onion over each serving.

Oyster Stew

4 pints oysters
1/2 cup finely chopped
    green onions
3 tablespoons butter
4 cups milk, lowfat
salt and cayenne to taste
Tabasco sauce to taste

Drain the oysters and check for shell pieces.

Sauté the green onions in the butter until the onions are soft. Add milk, salt, and pepper to the butter and green onions and heat. Add oysters and heat until the oyster begins to curl. Add Tabasco.

I have found that when I have to heat milk in a recipe, it helps to begin the heating process in the microwave. This keeps the milk from scorching on the bottom of the pan.

Shrimp and Okra Gumbo

3 pounds peeled shrimp
1 pound crab meat
1 bag crab boil
1/3 cup olive oil
4 cups fresh okra, sliced
2 large onions, chopped
1 large bell pepper,
    chopped
1 cup chopped celery
salt and cayenne to taste

In a large pot bring two quarts of water to boil. Put in crab boil, shrimp and crabmeat. Simmer for fifteen minutes.

In a skillet, sauté the cleaned, sliced okra in the olive oil. Cook over low heat until very tender. Add onions, bell pepper, and chopped celery and cook until the bell pepper is tender and clear. Remove from heat. Take the bag of crab boil out of the shrimp pot and add the okra mixture to the pot. Season to taste with salt and pepper. Simmer for 30 minutes. Serve over hot brown Basmati rice.

Zucchini Soup

4 cups diced zucchini
1 medium onion, chopped
2 cans chicken broth
1 bay leaf
1 cup milk
1 teaspoon Worcestershire
    sauce
salt and pepper to taste
boiled shrimp or crabmeat
(optional)

In a pot, bring the zucchini, onion, and chicken broth to boil. Add the bay leaf and simmer covered for twenty-five minutes. Remove from heat and remove the bay leaf. Place the mixture in a blender or food processor and whirl until smooth. Return the mixture to the pot and add the milk, Worcestershire sauce, salt and pepper, and shrimp or crabmeat (optional). Heat without boiling.

Broccoli Soup

2 tablespoons stone ground
   whole grain flour
2 tablespoons olive oil
2 large onions, chopped
1 large bell pepper,
   chopped
2 teaspoons minced garlic
1/2 cup chopped parsley
1/2 cup chopped celery
2 quarts canned chicken
   broth or water &
   bouillon crystals
2 packages frozen chopped
   broccoli
salt and pepper to taste

Make a roux with the flour and olive oil and sauté the onions, bell pepper, garlic, parsley, and celery in it until they are tender. Add the chicken broth, garlic, and parsley. Simmer for 45 minutes. Add broccoli and cook for 20 more minutes. Season to taste.

Variation: Add some stone ground whole grain pasta to the soup about ten minutes before it is finished cooking.

Cream of Crab Soup

3 stalks celery, chopped
   fine
1 large onion, chopped
4 tablespoons butter
1/2 cup stone ground whole
   grain flour
3 cups lowfat milk
1 pound crabmeat
salt and pepper to taste
nutmeg
chopped parsley

Sauté celery and onions in butter until tender. Blend in the flour. Add the milk slowly, blending well. Cook until the mixture thickens a little. Add the crabmeat and salt and pepper to taste. Cook on low heat for fifteen minutes, stirring often. Do not allow the milk to scorch on the bottom of the pan.

Garnish each bowl with a little nutmeg and parsley before serving.

Bucktown Bisque

1/2 cup olive oil
1/2 cup chopped onion
1 cup chopped celery
1 cup chopped green
    onions
1 quart chicken broth
1 cup chopped parsley
3 teaspoons salt
1 teaspoon black pepper
1/2 teaspoon thyme
4 bay leaves
Tabasco sauce to taste
3 pounds fish, cut into
    chunks
4 1/2 cups lowfat milk
1/3 cup stone ground whole
    grain flour
3 1/2 cups light cream
1 pound cooked shrimp,
    chopped
1 pound crabmeat
paprika

In a very large soup pot, sauté the onion, celery, and the green onion in the olive oil until tender. Add the broth, parsley, salt, pepper, thyme, bay leaves, Tabasco, and fish. Simmer for forty-five minutes.

In a small bowl, blend one cup of the milk with the flour until smooth. Stir this mixture into the soup, blending well. Slowly stir the rest of the milk and cream into the soup. Simmer over low heat, stirring, until the mixture thickens. Add the shrimp and crabmeat and cook for another ten minutes. Garnish each plate with paprika.

If you order courtbouillon (pronounced coo'-bee-yong but with the "g" silent) in a classic restaurant in France you get a rather thin sort of fish stock. Eat it in New Orleans and just see what the Creoles and Cajuns have done with it! Instead of a thin fish stock, they've turned it in to a robust, rich, aromatic fish stew.

Green Onion and Mushroom Soup

3 bunches green onions,
  chopped
1 pound fresh mushrooms,
  1/2 chopped,
  1/2 sliced
3 tablespoons butter
salt and black pepper
  to taste
cayenne pepper to taste
3 tablespoons stone ground
  whole grain flour
5 cups chicken broth
1 cup water
1/3 cup light sour cream

In a large soup pot, sauté the green onions and the chopped mushrooms in the butter until tender. Add the salt, pepper, and cayenne. Blend in the flour. Add one cup of the broth, stirring to blend. In a blender, puree this mixture and then return it to the pot. Slowly blend in the rest of the broth and the water. Add the sliced mushrooms and simmer for fifteen minutes. Add the sour cream and heat, but do not boil.

Turkey and Oyster Gumbo

Leftover turkey carcass
  with meat
5 chicken bouillon cubes
4 tablespoons olive oil
3 tablespoons stone ground
  whole grain flour
2 large onions, chopped
3 stalks celery, chopped
salt and pepper to taste
Tabasco to taste
1 quart oysters with liquid,
  checked for shell pieces
1 quart oysters with liquid,
  checked for shell pieces

In a large pot, cover turkey carcass with water, add the bouillon cubes, and boil for one hour. Remove and discard bones.

In a large pot, make a roux with the olive oil and flour and brown. Sauté the onions and celery in the roux until the onions are translucent. Add the turkey broth, turkey meat, salt, pepper, and Tabasco and simmer for one and a half hours. Add oysters and oyster liquid and cook for another twenty minutes. Serve over a little brown Basmati rice.

If the gumbo needs it, add a little Kitchen Bouquet to correct the color to a rich brown.

Broccoli and Crab Soup

1 bunch green onions,
    chopped
1 pound fresh mushrooms,
    chopped
2 cups fresh broccoli,
    chopped
1 1/2 teaspoon minced
    garlic
3 tablespoons butter
1/2 cup stone ground whole
    grain flour
salt and pepper to taste
2 cups lowfat milk
2 cans chicken broth
1 1/2 cups Swiss or gruyere
    cheese, grated
1 pound crabmeat

In a large pot, sauté the onions, mushrooms, broccoli, and garlic in the butter until tender. Blend in the flour, salt, and pepper. Stir in the milk slowly, blending well. Add the broth and cook, stirring, until the mixture thickens. Add the cheese and cook until melted. Add the crabmeat, first making sure there are no shell pieces. Cook for ten minutes or until thoroughly heated.

White Bean Soup

2 cups dried white beans
4 quarts water
2 cups chopped celery
4 cups chopped onion
1 cup chopped parsley
2 tablespoons no-sugar-
    tomato paste
2 tablespoons oregano
1/4 cup wine vinegar
salt and pepper to taste
Tabasco to taste

Put the beans, water, celery, and onion into a large soup pot and bring to a boil. Simmer for one hour.

Add the parsley, tomato paste, oregano, vinegar, salt, pepper, and Tabasco and simmer for two more hours.

Serve hot.

Louisiana Red Bean Soup

2 tablespoons olive oil
3 cloves garlic, chopped
2 large onions, chopped
2 ribs celery, chopped
1/2 cup parsley, chopped
1/2 pound lean ham or 1/2
    cup tasso, cut in 1/2"
    cubes
3 cans red beans with liquid
3 cans chicken broth
3 cups water
3 bay leaves
salt and pepper to taste
Tabasco to taste

In a large, heavy pot, sauté garlic, onions, celery, and parsley in olive oil until they are tender. Add meat and brown.

Put half of the beans with liquid into the blender and whirl. Leave only a little "chunkiness."

Add beans, broth, water, bay leaves, salt and pepper to the pot and cook covered for approximately half an hour. The soup should have a creamy consistency. If it is too thin, simmer for a while uncovered.

Add Tabasco to taste.

Chilled Avocado Soup

2 avocados
1/2 teaspoon fresh lemon
    juice
2 cups chicken broth
1 cup light cream
salt to taste
cayenne pepper

Peel and pit avocados. Puree in a blender with lemon juice. Blend in chicken broth. Pour into a bowl and whisk in cream. Season to taste with salt and cayenne. Chill.

Mock Hollandaise Sauce

1/2 cup Neufchatel cheese
3 tablespoons low fat
    yogurt
juice of 1/2 lemon
Salt and pepper to taste

Mix all ingredients in a food processor or blender until smooth. In a double boiler, cook over simmering water until hot and thick. Serve immediately or refrigerate and serve cold. Stir before using.

Variations: You can turn this into mock Béarnaise by adding a little tarragon and green onion. Turn it into mock mayonnaise by adding a little Dijon mustard and a little sugar substitute.

Simple Mayonnaise

2 egg yolks
1/2 teaspoon salt
1/4 teaspoon white pepper
1/2 teaspoon dry mustard
3 tablespoons tarragon
    vinegar
1 ½ cups olive oil

Beat egg yolks until thick and lighter in color. Beat in the salt, pepper, dry mustard and half of the vinegar. While beating, slowly add part of the olive oil, some vinegar, and then some more olive oil. After you have blended in the last of the olive oil, add the last of the vinegar only if the mayonnaise needs to be thinned a little.

Simple Mayonnaise II

2 eggs
2 teaspoons salt
2 packets sugar substitute
2 teaspoons dry mustard
3 cups olive oil
1 tablespoon lemon juice
red pepper to taste
Tabasco sauce to taste

Put the eggs, salt, sweetener, and dry mustard in a blender or in a bowl for the electric mixer. Mix until well blended. Add the olive oil in a steady stream while mixing. Add lemon juice, pepper, and Tabasco. Cover and refrigerate.

Sour Cream Sauce

1 cup sour cream, light
1 teaspoon lemon juice
1 tablespoon horseradish
2 teaspoons chives,
    chopped fine
2 teaspoons minced onion
2 teaspoons green onions,
    chopped fine
1/2 cup no-sugar-added
    mayonnaise,
1/4 teaspoon mustard
    powder

Mix all ingredients and chill well. This is great for boiled seafood.

Tarragon Mayonnaise

1 raw egg
1 tablespoon Dijon mustard
1 tablespoon vinegar
1 teaspoon lemon juice
1 ½ teaspoons dried
    tarragon
1/2 teaspoon pepper
1/4 teaspoon salt
3/4 cup olive oil

In a blender, mix the egg, mustard, vinegar, lemon juice, tarragon, pepper, and salt well. With the blender running, add the olive oil in a slow stream and whirl until the mixture thickens. Pour into a jar or bowl and refrigerate.

You can use this mayo in just about any recipe that calls for sugar free mayonnaise.

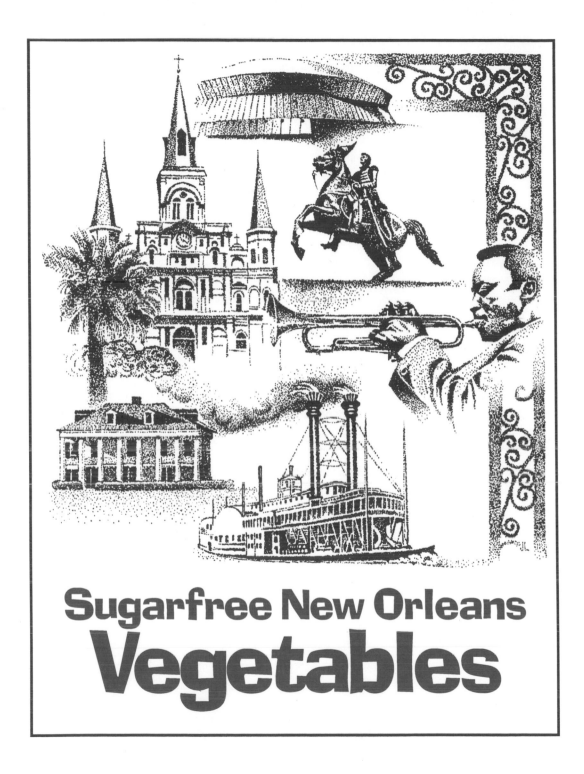

Sugarfree New Orleans
Vegetables

Artichoke and Mushroom Casserole

2 cans artichoke hearts,
    well drained
1 pound fresh mushrooms
3/4 stick butter
1 carton light sour cream
1 teaspoon Worcestershire
    sauce
1 tablespoon parsley
salt and pepper to taste
Tabasco sauce to taste
1/2 cup Parmesan cheese

Squeeze as much water as possible from the artichoke hearts. Cut into quarters and place into casserole dish. Clean the mushrooms and pat dry. If the mushrooms are larger than bite size, cut them. Sauté the mushrooms in the butter for about 10 minutes. Remove them with a slotted spoon to the casserole dish.

Add the sour cream to the remaining margarine in the pan and blend well. Add the Worcestershire sauce, parsley, salt, pepper, and Tabasco and mix well. Pour this mixture into the casserole dish over the artichokes and mushrooms. Sprinkle with Parmesan cheese. Bake at 350F for thirty minutes or until bubbly.

Artichoke Pie

1 can artichoke hearts
lemon juice
3 tablespoons olive oil
stone ground whole grain
    flour
4 eggs
garlic salt and pepper
    to taste
2 tablespoons lowfat milk

Drain the artichoke hearts well and slice vertically in rounds. Lay the slices out on paper toweling and pat dry. Sprinkle with lemon juice. Toss the artichoke hearts in flour and sauté in hot olive oil until light brown on both sides. Place the artichokes and the olive oil in a pie plate.

In a bowl, beat the eggs with the salt, pepper, and milk. Pour over the artichoke hearts and olive oil. Pour into a greased pie plate and bake in a preheated 350F degree oven until the egg mixture is set — about ten minutes.

Artichoke Quiche Squares

2 cans marinated artichoke
    hearts
1/4 cup minced onion
1 clove garlic, minced
1/4 teaspoon oregano
2 tablespoons parsley
    chopped fine
4 eggs
1/4 cup crushed stone
    ground crackers
1/4 teaspoon salt
1/4 teaspoon black pepper
Tabasco sauce to taste
2 cups grated Cheddar
    cheese

Drain the artichoke hearts reserving liquid. Chop the artichokes very fine and set aside.

In a small saucepan cook the onions, garlic, oregano, and parsley in about half of the reserved marinade over medium heat for 5 minutes. Remove from heat and set aside.

In a bowl, beat the eggs until blended. Add chopped artichokes, cracker crumbs, salt, pepper, and Tabasco and mix well. Stir in the cheddar cheese and the cooked marinade mixture.

Pour into a greased 9x9 inch baking pan. Bake at 325F (300F if using a glass pan) for 35 to 40 minutes or until firm.

Cut into large squares to serve as a vegetable for dinner or into small squares to use as appetizers. This dish freezes well.

Artichokes au Vin

4 fresh artichokes
10 whole small onions
1 cup white wine
1 cup water
1/4 cup olive oil
1 bay leaf
1/4 cup chopped parsley
1 tablespoon lemon juice

Clean the artichokes and cut in quarters. Remove the inner prickly part.

In a large pot combine all of the ingredients. Bring to a boil and simmer, covered, until the artichokes are tender. Artichokes are done when a leaf pulls out easily.

Baked Parmesan Onions

4 medium onions
4 tablespoons butter,
    softened
4 tablespoons Worcester-
    shire sauce
1/2 teaspoon tarragon
salt and pepper to taste
1/3 cup grated fresh
    Parmesan cheese

Cut four large squares of heavy-duty aluminum foil. Each should be large enough to seal an entire onion.

In a small bowl, blend the butter with the Worcestershire sauce, tarragon, salt, pepper, and Parmesan.

Peel skin from onion and then make an "X" cut almost all the way through. Place each onion on a square of foil. Spread the onions open enough to spoon in the butter mixture.

Wrap and seal each onion with foil and bake at 350F for one hour.

Cheddar Onions

6 medium onions
1 1/2 cups shredded
    Cheddar cheese
1/2 teaspoon thyme
1/2 teaspoon salt
1/4 teaspoon pepper
1 can chicken broth

Cut a slice off both ends of each onion and peel. Scoop out the center of each onion, being sure to leave the bottom intact. Leave a 3 ring thick onion shell.

Chop the removed centers and mix with the cheese, thyme, salt, and pepper.

Fill each onion with the cheese mixture and place in a baking pan. Pour about 1/2 inch of chicken broth in the bottom of the pan. Bake for one hour and fifteen minutes at 400F. If the pan starts to dry out, add a little more chicken broth.

White Beans D. Ray

1 pound white beans
1/3 cup chopped bell
  pepper
1/3 cup chopped celery
1 onion, chopped
2 teaspoons minced garlic
2 tablespoons olive oil
1/2 cup diced very lean ham
2 bay leaves
2 tablespoons Worcester-
  shire sauce
salt and pepper to taste

Soak beans in water for at least six hours; overnight is even better. Rinse and drain.

In a heavy pot, sauté the bell pepper, celery, onion, and garlic in the olive oil until tender. Add the beans, ham, bay leaves, Worcestershire sauce, salt, and pepper and enough hot water to cover.

Cover the pot and simmer for at least two hours or until beans are tender.

White Beans Delphi

3 cups dried white beans
1/2 cup olive oil
2 onions, chopped
2 celery stalks, choppd
1 teaspoon minced garlic
8 ounces no-sugar-added
  tomato sauce
2 bay leaves
1 teaspoon oregano
salt and pepper to taste

Put beans in a large pot, cover with water, and simmer for 3 hours. Drain.

In the pot, sauté the onions and celery in the olive oil until tender. Add the garlic, tomato sauce, bay leaves, oregano, salt, and pepper. Simmer for ten minutes. If the sauce gets too thick, add a little hot water. Return the beans to the pot, cover, and simmer for twenty minutes.

Bayou Broccoli

2 bunches fresh broccoli
1 tablespoon olive oil
3 tablespoons stone ground
    whole grain flour
3/4 cup chicken broth
1/2 cup lowfat milk
1/4 teaspoon garlic powder
salt and pepper to taste
1/3 cup sugarfree
    mayonnaise
1 tablespoon lemon juice
1/2 cup grated Cheddar
    cheese

Cut broccoli into chunks and steam until tender but still crisp. Place the broccoli into an ovenproof casserole dish.

In a saucepan, blend the olive oil and flour. Stir in the broth and the milk gradually, blending well. Cook until the mixture comes to a boil and thickens a little. Stir constantly. Add the garlic, salt, and pepper. Remove the pan from the heat and blend in the mayonnaise, lemon juice, and cheese. Pour this mixture over the broccoli and bake the casserole at 350F for twenty minutes or until bubbly.

Broccoli di Firenze

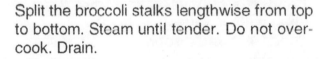

1 pound fresh broccoli,
    washed and trimmed
2 tablespoons olive oil
2 cloves garlic, sliced
salt and pepper to taste

Split the broccoli stalks lengthwise from top to bottom. Steam until tender. Do not overcook. Drain.

In a large skillet sauté the garlic in olive oil until the garlic is tender. Toss the broccoli gently in the garlic oil to coat. Sprinkle lightly with salt and pepper.

Irish Channel Baked Tomatoes

4 large ripe tomatoes
3 tablespoons butter,
    softened
1/2 teaspoon salt
1/4 teaspoon black pepper
1 teaspoon garlic powder
1 teaspoon ground
    coriander
1 teaspoon ground cumin
1/2 teaspoon oregano

Mix softened butter with the salt, pepper, garlic powder, coriander, cumin, and oregano. Blend well.

Clean tomatoes and cut in half. Spread the butter mixture gently on the cut surface of the tomatoes. Place in a baking dish in a 325F oven for 25 minutes.

Veggie Stuffed Tomatoes

6 medium tomatoes
2 tablespoons olive oil
1 medium zucchini,
    chopped in chunks
1 medium yellow squash
1/4 pound fresh mushrooms
1/3 cup onions
1 teaspoon minced garlic
1 teaspoon basil
Parmesan cheese, grated

Cut a large slice off the top of each tomato and discard. Scoop out the tomato, saving the pulp and the juice. Place the tomatoes face down to drain.

In a skillet, sauté the tomato pulp, zucchini, squash, mushrooms, onions, garlic, and basil in olive oil until the vegetables are tender. Add a little of the tomato juice as you are cooking. Spoon the mixture into the tomato shells and sprinkle with Parmesan. Bake the tomatoes at 350F for 20 minutes.

Horseradish Green Beans

2 cans green beans
1 onion, sliced thin
1/4 pound lean ham chunks
1 cup no-sugar-added
    mayonnaise
2 hardboiled eggs, chopped
1 tablespoon horseradish
1 teaspoon Worcestershire
    sauce
1/8 teaspoon garlic powder
1 teaspoon chopped
    parsley
1 tablespoon lemon juice
salt and pepper to taste

Simmer the beans, covered, with their liquid, the onion, and ham chunks for 1 hour.

Blend mayonnaise with the eggs, horseradish, Worcestershire sauce, garlic, parsley, lemon juice, salt, and pepper.

When ready to serve, drain the beans and spoon the sauce over the top.

This is also good served cold.

Basil Green Beans

1 1/2 pounds fresh green
    beans
salt
1/4 cup chopped onion
2 tablespoons olive oil
2 tablespoons chopped
    basil leaves
salt and pepper to taste
3 tablespoons vinegar

Wash beans and snap off ends. Boil in a large pot of salted water for ten minutes. Drain.

In a large saucepan, sauté the onion in olive oil until tender. Add the beans, basil leaves, salt, pepper, and vinegar. Stir beans to coat. Serve hot.

Herbed Brussels Sprouts

2 pounds fresh Brussels
　　Sprouts
1/3 cup olive oil
1 tablespoon minced onion
1 tablespoon lemon juice
1/4 teaspoon salt
1/4 teaspoon thyme
1/4 teaspoon marjoram

Cook Brussels sprouts in boiling water until tender. Drain.

In a saucepan, sauté the onion in olive oil until tender. Add the lemon juice, salt, thyme, and marjoram. Pour over the drained Brussels sprouts and toss to coat.

Creamy Green Beans

2 cans green beans
8 ounces light cream
　　cheese
1/2 teaspoon salt
1/4 teaspoon black pepper
1/2 teaspoon garlic salt
1/2 cup Parmesan cheese

In a large saucepan, combine the cream cheese, salt, pepper, garlic salt and Parmesan cheese. Cook on medium heat, stirring, until cheese melts thoroughly. Drain green beans well and add to sauce. Serve hot.

Asparagus Lafayette

1 1/2 pounds fresh
　　asparagus
1 red bell pepper
1 cup chicken broth
salt to taste

Clean asparagus and trim the stalks. Cut the pepper into thin strips, discarding the seeds and trimming the inside. Simmer the asparagus and pepper strips in about one inch of chicken stock until tender. Serve asparagus and peppers together.

Loretta's Mixed Greens

2 bunches mustard greens
2 bunches turnip greens
1 medium onion, chopped
3 tablespoons olive oil
1 teaspoon vinegar
salt and pepper to taste
Tabasco sauce to taste

Clean greens really well, rinsing several times and tearing into pieces. Drain. In a large heavy pot, sauté the onion in olive oil until tender. Put the greens into the pot with a few spoons of water, cover tightly and cook for ten minutes. Add vinegar, salt, pepper, and Tabasco and stir well. Cover and cook on medium low heat for 50 minutes or until tender. Stir frequently, adding a little hot water if necessary.

Do not use the turnips themselves. They are really high on the Glycemic Index.

Louisiana Red Beans

2 cups dried red beans, washed and dried
6 cups water
1/2 pound lean ham or 1/2 cup tasso, cut in 1" cubes
2 tablespoons olive oil
3 cloves garlic, chopped
2 large onions, chopped
2 ribs celery, chopped
1/2 cup parsley, chopped
3 bay leaves
salt and pepper to taste

In a large, heavy pot, sauté the garlic, onions, celery, and parsley in olive oil until they are wilted. Add meat and brown slightly. Add beans, water, bay leaves, salt and pepper and cook uncovered for approximately four hours or until beans are tender. Beans should remain covered with water during the cooking process. Serve over brown Basmati rice. The cooked red beans freeze well.

Mushrooms Florentine

1 pound fresh mushrooms
2 packages frozen chopped
    spinach
1 small onion, chopped fine
1/2 teaspoon minced garlic
1/2 cup olive oil
1 carton light sour cream
1/4 teaspoon nutmeg
1 1/2 teaspoons salt
1/4 teaspoon pepper
1/3 cup Parmesan cheese

Clean mushrooms and pat dry. Trim and cut into bite sized pieces. Set aside.

In a large saucepan, cook the spinach according to directions, using half of the salt. Pour the spinach into a colander and drain well.

Return the pan to the stove and sauté the mushrooms, onion, and garlic in the olive oil for ten minutes or until tender. Add the sour cream, nutmeg, salt, pepper, and Parmesan cheese. Blend well.

Squeeze as much liquid as possible out of the spinach and then add it to the mushrooms and sauce. Heat thoroughly and serve.

Mushrooms in Sour Cream

1 pound fresh mushrooms
1 onion, coarsely chopped
1/4 cup chopped green
    onions, chopped
1/2 stick butter
1 cup low fat sour cream
2 tablespoons vermouth
    (optional)
1 teaspoon salt
1/2 teaspoon pepper

Clean mushrooms, trim stems, and slice in half. Pat dry.

Sauté onions and green onions in butter until limp. Add mushrooms, cover and cook on low heat for 5 minutes. Stir in sour cream, vermouth, salt, and pepper. Simmer for 5 more minutes.

Great served with lean steak and other meats.

Parmesan Zucchini

5 medium zucchini
2/3 cup grated, fresh Parmesan cheese
1/2 cup crumbs from stone ground whole grain bread
1/2 teaspoon garlic powder
1/2 teaspoon sage
2 eggs
1 tablespoon olive oil
salt and pepper to taste

Wash zucchini and trim the ends off. Cut lengthwise into long quarters. Set aside.

In a large bowl, combine Parmesan, breadcrumbs, garlic powder, and sage. In another long bowl, beat the eggs. One strip at a time, dip the zucchini into the egg to coat. Let the excess egg drip off and then roll the zucchini strip in the cheese mixture to coat.

Put the strips in a greased baking pan and sprinkle with olive oil, salt, and pepper.

Bake at 425F for 25 minutes.

Ratatouille

1 medium onion, chopped
1 bell pepper, chopped
2 teaspoons minced garlic
2 tablespoons olive oil
1 large can whole tomatoes
1 medium eggplant, cut in chunks
3 medium zucchini, cut in chunks
1 medium bell pepper, chopped
salt and pepper to taste
1/3 cup sliced ripe olives

Sauté the onion, bell pepper, and garlic in the olive oil until tender. Add the tomatoes and let simmer for ten minutes. Add the eggplant and the zucchini (skins on), bell pepper, salt, and pepper. Cook until the eggplant is tender. Remove from heat and add the olives. This can be served hot or cold.

Smothered Cabbage

1 head cabbage, cut up
3 tablespoons olive oil
1 medium onion, chopped
1/3 pound lean ham chunks
salt and pepper to taste

Heat olive oil in a heavy pot. Sauté onions until almost tender. Add ham chunks and brown. Add washed cabbage, salt and pepper and about 1/2 inch of water. Cover and cook over medium heat for one hour, stirring occasionally. If your pot top is not tight enough, you may have to occasionally add a little hot water.

Caraway Cabbage

2 pounds cabbage
4 cups boiling water
1 cup sour cream
1 teaspoon caraway seeds
salt and pepper to taste

Cut cabbage into small chunks and boil until tender. Drain well and put back into pot. Add sour cream, caraway, salt, and pepper. Heat thoroughly, but do not let the sour cream boil.

Notes:

_____
_____
_____
_____
_____
_____
_____
_____
_____
_____

Cabbage Clovis

1 cabbage, cut in wedges
1/4 cup chopped bell
    pepper
1/2 cup chopped onion
1/2 cup celery
1/4 cup olive oil
1/4 cup stone ground whole
    grain flour
1/2 teaspoon salt
1/4 teaspoon pepper
Tabasco sauce to taste
1 1/2 cups lowfat milk
1/2 sugarfree mayonnaise
1/2 cup grated Cheddar
    cheese
3 tablespoons sugarfree
    chili sauce

Cook the cabbage in water until it is just tender. Do not overcook. Drain the cabbage and place in an ovenproof casserole dish.

Sauté the onions and celery in the olive oil until tender and then blend in the flour. Add salt, pepper, and Tabasco. Add milk a little at a time and blend until smooth. When the milk begins to bubble and thicken, pour it over the cabbage and bake at 375F for twenty minutes. Combine the mayonnaise, cheese, and chili sauce. Spread this over the cabbage and bake for 10 more minutes or until the cheese is melted and bubbly.

Cream Cheese Spinach

3 boxes frozen spinach
1/2 stick butter
1/4 cup olive oil
1/2 cup chopped onions
1/4 cup chopped parsley,
1/2 teaspoon mince garlic
8 ounces low fat cream
    cheese
2 tablespoons Worcester-
    shire sauce
salt and pepper to taste
Tabasco sauce to taste

Allow spinach to thaw and drain.

In a large saucepan, melt butter with the olive oil and sauté the onion, parsley, and garlic until tender. Cut the cream cheese into chunks and add to the pan. On medium heat, melt the cream cheese. Squeeze all of the liquid out of the spinach and put it into the pan. Add the Worcestershire sauce, salt, pepper, and Tabasco. Pour this mixture into an ovenproof casserole dish and bake at 350F for 30 minutes or until it is bubbling hot.

Spicy Spinach

2 packages frozen chopped
    spinach
4 tablespoons olive oil
1 small onion, chopped
2 tablespoons stone ground
    whole grain flour
1/2 cup spinach liquid
1/2 cup evaporated skim
    milk
1/2 pound jalapeno cheese
    cut in chunks
1/4 teaspoon black pepper
1/4 teaspoon red pepper
1/2 teaspoon celery salt
1 teaspoon Worcestershire
    sauce

Cook spinach as directed on box. Drain but save the liquid. Set aside.

Sauté the onion in the olive oil in a large pot until the onion is tender. Blend in the flour. Add the spinach liquid slowly while blending. Add the evaporated milk and cook, stirring continuously, until the sauce thickens. Add the cheese and stir until it is melted. Stir in the pepper, salt, and Worcestershire sauce. Add the drained spinach and stir until well blended.

Serve immediately from the stove or put the mixture into a casserole dish to bake later for 20 minutes at 350F.

Spinach and Artichoke Casserole

1 jar marinated artichoke
    hearts, drained and
    chopped
2 packages frozen chopped
    spinach, thawed
8 ounces light cream
    cheese, softened
2 tablespoons olive oil
pepper to taste
4 tablespoons milk
1/2 cup grated Parmesan
    cheese

Arrange artichoke hearts across the bottom of a casserole dish. Cover evenly with the uncooked spinach that has been squeezed dry. In a small bowl, beat the cream cheese, olive oil, and pepper until well blended. Add the milk, a bit at a time, and continue to beat. Spread this mixture over the spinach. Sprinkle the Parmesan evenly over the top.

Bake at 350F for 30 minutes covered. Remove cover and bake for 10 more minutes.

Spinach with Sour Cream

2 boxes frozen chopped
    spinach
1 tablespoon minced onion
3 eggs
3/4 cup light sour cream
1 cup grated fresh Par-
    mesan cheese
1 tablespoon stone ground
    whole grain flour
1 tablespoon olive oil
salt and pepper to taste

Cook the spinach in water with the onion. Drain well and squeeze out excess liquid when the spinach is cool enough. In a large bowl, beat the eggs and add the sour cream, Parmesan, flour, olive oil. Mix well. Stir in the spinach and add salt and pepper to taste.

Pour the mixture into a greased casserole dish and bake at 350F for 30 minutes.

Squash Bake

3 cups sliced yellow squash
3 cups sliced zucchini
1 medium onion, chopped
1/2 cup chopped celery
1 medium bell pepper,
    chopped
1/2 cup olive oil
8 ounces light sour cream
1 egg, beaten
1/3 cup crushed stone
    ground crackers
1 cup shredded cheddar
    cheese

Cook the yellow squash and the zucchini in lightly salted water until tender. Drain well and set aside.

In a large skillet, sauté the onion, celery and bell pepper in the olive oil until they turn clear. Remove from heat and slowly stir in the sour cream, blending well. Mix in the egg, 1/2 of the crushed crackers, and the cheddar. Stir the mixture well and then fold in the yellow squash and the zucchini.

Pour the whole mixture into a greased casserole dish and sprinkle the remaining crushed Triscuits over the top. Bake at 350F for 30 minutes.

Squash Rockefeller

6 yellow squash
2 boxes frozen chopped
    spinach
1 bunch green onions,
    chopped
1/2 cup chopped parsley
1 teaspoon minced garlic
3 tablespoons olive oil
1/3 cup crushed stone
    ground crackers
salt and pepper to taste
Parmesan cheese, grated

Wash squash and cut in half lengthwise. Steam in a little water, covered, until tender. Let the squash cool and then carefully scoop out the seeds and discard.

Cook the spinach according to package directions and drain well. Squeeze out as much liquid as possible.

In a pan, sauté the green onion, parsley, and garlic in the olive oil until tender. Add the spinach, crushed crackers, salt and pepper and stir well.

Stuff this mixture into the squash shells. Sprinkle with Parmesan and bake at 350F for twenty minutes.

When the Ursuline nuns arrived in New Orleans in 1730, a treaty was signed giving them enough room in the city to plant an herb garden. The old Ursulines cookbook notes that "few truly Creole dishes can be prepared without some variant of herb bouquet to accentuate flavor and bring out the special delicacy of the central ingredient."

Squash Squares

3 cups yellow squash,
    chopped
1/4 cup olive oil
1 medium onion, chopped
    fine
1/2 teaspoon minced garlic
6 eggs
1/3 cup crumbled stone
    ground crackers
1/2 teaspoon oregano
1/2 teaspoon salt
1/2 teaspoon pepper
3 cups cheddar cheese
    coarse grated
1/2 cup grated, fresh Par-
    mesan cheese

Cook onions in olive oil in a large frying pan until tender. Add garlic and squash and cook, stirring for about 4 more minutes or until the squash is tender. Set the pan aside.

In a large bowl, combine the eggs, Triscuit crumbs, oregano, salt, pepper, and cheddar cheese. Mix this together well and then stir in the squash mixture. Turn the mixture out into a greased casserole dish (9"x13" should work well). Use a smaller dish if you want the squares thicker. Sprinkle with Parmesan cheese.

Bake at 325F for thirty minutes or until the center part of the squash squares feels set. Let cool for about ten minutes before cutting the squares and serving.

Notes:

Aubergines St. Rémy

2 eggplants
2 onions, sliced thin
1 large can of whole
　　tomatoes with juice
1 teaspoon oregano
1/2 teaspoon basil
salt and pepper to taste
1/2 pound mozzarella
　　cheese, shredded

Peel the eggplants and slice into 1/2" rounds. Broil the eggplant until the top side is light brown – about five minutes. Place the eggplant, brown side down into a greased casserole dish. Spread the sliced onions over it.

Drain the tomatoes, saving the juice. Chop the tomatoes very fine and put them into a bowl. Add the juice, oregano, basil, salt, and pepper and mix well. Pour this over the eggplant and onions. Bake for 50 minutes at 350F. Top with the mozzarella cheese and bake for another ten minutes or until the cheese is melted.

Eggplant and Olives

1 large eggplant
1 bell pepper, chopped
2 ribs celery, chopped
1 onion, chopped
1/4 stick butter
3 tablespoons olive oil
1 teaspoon Worcester-
　　shire sauce
1 cup shredded Cheddar
　　cheese
1 cup ripe olives, chopped
salt and pepper to taste
Tabasco sauce to taste

Peel the eggplant and chop into big bite sized chunks. Steam until tender. In a large skillet, cook the bell pepper, celery, and onion in the butter and olive oil until they are translucent. Add the cooked eggplant, the Worcestershire sauce, cheese, and olives. Stir well to combine. Taste before adding salt, pepper, and Tabasco.

Turn the mixture into an ovenproof casserole dish and bake at 375F for thirty minutes.

Stuffed Eggplant

2 medium eggplants
2 tablespoons chopped
    parsley
1/2 cup chopped green
    onions
4 tablespoons olive oil
1 cup chopped boiled
    shrimp
salt and pepper to taste
grated fresh Parmesan
    cheese

Cut eggplants in half lengthwise. Place in a baking pan with about 1/2" water. Bake in a preheated 350F oven for about ten minutes or until tender. Scoop out all of the pulp and put it aside. Keep the shells for stuffing.

In a large skillet, sauté the parsley and green onion in the olive oil. Add the shrimp and the eggplant pulp. Season with salt and pepper and stir well. Cook for five minutes on medium heat, stirring often so that the bottom does not scorch. Fill the eggplant shells with the mixture and top with grated Parmesan. Bake at 350F until the top begins to brown.

Stewed Cauliflower

1 head cauliflower
1/2 cup olive oil
1 onion, chopped
1/2 teaspoon minced garlic
1 bay leaf
1 tablespoon vinegar
1/4 cup chopped parsley

Clean cauliflower and trim off the tough stem. You can leave the cauliflower whole or break into pieces.

In a pot, sauté the onion and garlic in the olive oil until tender. Add bay leaf, vinegar, parsley, cauliflower, and enough hot water to cover the cauliflower. Simmer covered for fifteen minutes or until tender.

Yams Evelyn

3 sweet potatoes, peeled
    and sliced 1/4" thick
3 slices bacon
cinnamon

Fry bacon, remove from pan, drain, and crumble. Pour out most of the bacon grease leaving a thin coating in the pan.

Put a layer of yams in the pan and sprinkle with cinnamon and crumbled bacon. Add more layers. Add only enough water to cover the bottom layer of yams. Simmer, covered, about twenty minutes or until tender, flipping occasionally.

Glazed Sweet Potatoes

2 1/2 pounds fresh sweet
    potatoes
1/2 stick butter
4 tablespoons brown sugar
    substitute
1/2 cup chopped pecans

Cut sweet potatoes in half crosswise. Place in large pot with enough lightly salted water to cover the potatoes. Boil until tender and then drain. When the potatoes have cooled, slice into 1/4" rounds.

In a greased casserole dish, layer the potatoes, pats of butter, and brown sugar until you have used them all. Sprinkle the chopped pecans across the top.

Bake at 350F for 25 minutes or until the pecans begin to brown.

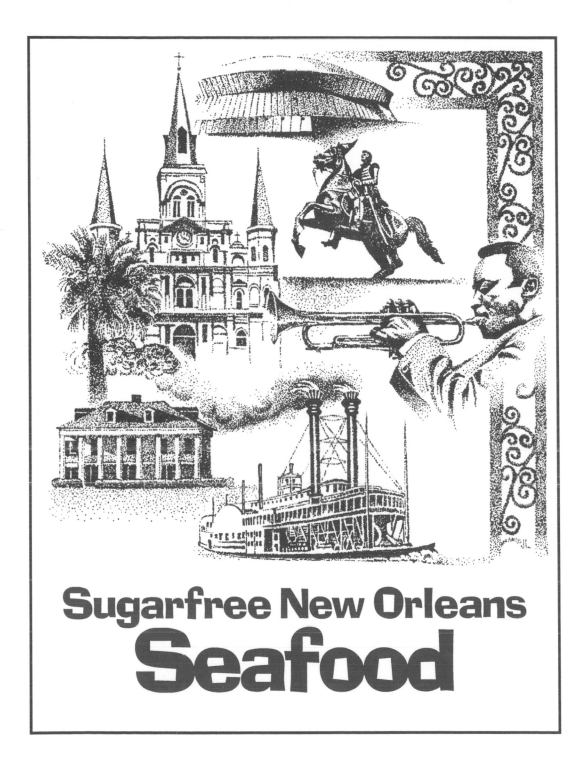

Sugarfree New Orleans
Seafood

Beth's Broiled Trout

6 large trout filets
salt and pepper to taste
cayenne to taste
1/2 stick butter
1/4 cup olive oil
2 teaspoons Worcestershire
    sauce
2 teaspoons lemon juice
1 ½ tablespoons chopped
    parsley
6 thin lemon slices

Rinse filets, pat dry and place on aluminum foil in a shallow pan. Sprinkle generously with the salt and peppers. Melt butter with olive oil, Worcestershire sauce, and lemon juice in a small saucepan. Pour half of the butter mixture over the fish and broil in a hot oven for six minutes. Center a lemon slice on each filet and pour on the rest of the butter sauce. Broil for six more minutes or until nicely browned. It is not necessary to turn the fish. Sprinkle the parsley over the fish and serve hot.

Variation: There are lots of fish that are delicious broiled this way - red snapper, bass, grouper, etc.

Crabmeat au Gratin

2 pounds fresh crabmeat
2 sticks butter
1 large onion, chopped fine
¼ cup green onion,
    chopped fine
3 stalks celery, chopped
    fine
4 tablespoons stone ground
    whole grain flour
1 ½ cans evaporated skim
    milk
2 egg yolks
salt and pepper to taste
2/3 pound mild Cheddar
    cheese grated

Pick crabmeat carefully to remove any shell pieces. Set aside.

Melt butter in a large pan and sauté the onions and celery until they are very tender. Do not brown. Add the flour and blend well. Add milk slowly while stirring. The sauce will thicken. Remove the pan from the heat and add the egg yolks, salt, pepper, and grated cheese. Pour the mixture into a casserole dish or into individual ramekins.

Bake at 350F for 30 minutes or until top begins to brown.

Crawfish au Gratin

1/2 cup olive oil
1 medium onion, chopped
1/3 cup celery, chopped fine
1/2 cup stone ground whole
  grain flour
1 1/2 cans evaporated skim
  milk
3 egg yolks
1 teaspoon salt
1/2 teaspoon black pepper
3 cups boiled crawfish tails
  (or shrimp)
3/4 pound cheddar cheese,
  shredded

In a large skillet, sauté the onions and celery in olive oil until they look clear. Add flour and stir well. Add milk a little at a time, blending well. Add egg yolks, salt, and pepper. Simmer for ten minutes, stirring often. Remove from heat and stir in half of the cheese. You do not need to melt the cheese. Place the crawfish tails in a greased casserole dish or in individual ramekins. Pour the sauce over the crawfish and top with the rest of the cheese.

Bake at 350F for twenty minutes or until cheese begins to brown.

Crawfish Etoufée

2 pounds peeled crawfish
  tails
1/4 cup olive oil
2 tablespoons stone ground
  whole grain flour
1 cup onions, chopped
2 gloves garlic, minced
1/2 cup green onion,
  chopped
1/4 cup parsley, chopped
1/2 teaspoon paprika
1 1/2 cups water
salt and pepper to taste
Tabasco sauce to taste

Make a roux by cooking the flour in the oil on medium heat until the mixture is nicely browned.

Caution: *stir constantly; a burned roux will ruin any dish.*

Sauté the onions, green onions, garlic, and parsley in the roux until tender. Add crawfish tails and sauté for 5 minutes. Add the salt & pepper, paprika, water, and Tabasco and stir well. Simmer for ten more minutes. Serve over hot brown Basmati rice.

Crawfish Jambalaya

1 pound peeled crawfish
    tails
4 cups cooked Basmati
    brown rice
1/2 stick butter
1/4 cup olive oil
2 teaspoons minced garlic
1 large onion, chopped
2 stalks celery, chopped
1 small bell pepper,
    chopped
1 bunch green onions,
    chopped
2 tablespoons chopped
    parsley
1/2 cup water
salt and cayenne pepper
    to taste

Melt butter in a large heavy pot with the olive oil. Sauté the garlic, onion, celery, and bell pepper until very tender. Add the crawfish, green onion, parsley, water, salt and pepper and cook covered for ten minutes, stirring occasionally. Add cooked rice and stir well. Put the top back on the pot and allow the jambalaya to steam on low heat for five minutes.

You can substitute stone ground whole grain pasta for the rice.

Crawfish Portofino

2 tablespoons olive oil
1 medium onion, chopped
    fine
1 pound fresh mushrooms,
    sliced
3 teaspoons minced garlic
1 pint light cream
2 pounds crawfish tails,
    uncooked
1/2 teaspoon oregano
1/3 cup no-sugar-added
    spaghetti sauce
salt and cayenne to taste

In a heavy pot, sauté the onions, mushrooms, and garlic in the olive oil. Slowly add the cream, blending well. Simmer uncovered for fifteen minutes, stirring often. Add crawfish, oregano, spaghetti sauce, salt, and pepper. Simmer, uncovered, for 20 minutes. Serve over stone ground whole grain pasta.

Garlic Shrimp

2 pounds shrimp, peeled
1/2 cup olive oil
1 teaspoon minced garlic
1/2 teaspoon salt
1/2 teaspoon pepper
2 tablespoons parsley,
    minced
2 tablespoons green onion,
    minced
1 tablespoon Worcester-
    shire sauce

Mix olive oil, garlic, salt, pepper, parsley, green onion, and Worcestershire sauce. Add shrimp and toss to coat. Cover, refrigerate, and allow to marinate overnight or at least for six hours.

Put shrimp and sauce in a large baking pan and bake at 375F for about 10-12 minutes. This can be served on stone ground whole grain pasta or with toothpicks as an appetizer.

Marinated Shrimp

1 cup olive oil
1/2 cup tarragon vinegar
1/2 teaspoon salt
2 tablespoons capers
2 teaspoons celery seeds
1 teaspoon black pepper
1 tablespoon soy sauce
Tabasco sauce to taste
2 pounds boiled shrimp,
    large peeled
2 large onions, sliced thin
6 bay leaves

In a large bowl, combine olive oil, vinegar, salt, capers, celery seeds, pepper, soy sauce and Tabasco. Mix well. Add shrimp, onions, and bay leaves. Stir all of this well, cover and refrigerate for 24 hours, stirring a couple of times during the marinating time. Drain and serve.

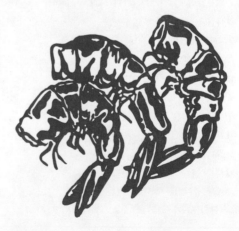

Oysters & Artichokes

4 fresh artichokes
4 dozen oysters
oyster liquid
2 tablespoons stone ground
   whole grain flour
1/2 cup olive oil
1/2 cup green onions
   chopped fine
1 1/2 teaspoons minced
   garlic
1 tablespoon lemon juice
1 tablespoon Worcester-
   shire sauce
1/3 cup parsley, chopped
   fine
dash thyme
salt and cayenne to taste
1/2 cup Parmesan cheese
1 large lemon
paprika

Boil the artichokes for 40 minutes or until a leaf comes out easily when you pull. Remove the leaves and scrape the inside of each leaf with a spoon to get the "meat". Clean the hearts and mash or chop them into small chunks. Set aside.

Drain the oysters, reserving the liquid and checking well for shell pieces.

In a large saucepan, blend the olive oil and flour. Sauté the green onions and garlic in the roux on medium heat. Add a little of the oyster liquid slowly, blending with the roux. Add the lemon juice, the Worcestershire sauce, parsley, thyme, salt and pepper and simmer uncovered for ten minutes. Add oysters and cook for about five minutes or until the sides of the oysters begin to curl. Add the artichoke "mash" and blend well. If the mixture is too thick, add a little more oyster liquid; if it is too thin, add some breadcrumbs made from whole grain bread or crushed stone ground crackers.

Pour the mixture into a greased casserole dish or into individual ramekins. Sprinkle generously with Parmesan cheese. Slice the lemon into thin rounds and distribute over the top. Sprinkle each lemon slice with paprika.

Bake at 400F for ten minutes or until top is bubbly.

Oysters Bienville

1 ½ pints oysters
1/4 cup olive oil
3 tablespoons whole grain
  flour, stone ground
2 cloves garlic, minced
1/4 cup onion, minced
1 small can mushroom
  pieces,
1/4 teaspoon celery seeds
1 tablespoon Worcester-
  shire sauce
1 ½ tablespoons white wine
3/4 cup oyster liquid
2 tablespoons paprika
salt and pepper to taste
1 dozen shrimp, cooked and
  chopped fine
1/2 cup Parmesan cheese

Drain oysters reserving liquid. Melt olive oil with flour and blend. Sauté garlic, onion and mushrooms for several minutes. Add celery seeds, Worcestershire sauce, wine, oyster liquid, salt and pepper, and paprika. Cook for several minutes until the mixture thickens. Add the chopped shrimp.

Place oysters on a pan and broil just until the edges begin to curl. Pour off the liquid and place oysters on shells or in individual ramekins. Sprinkle the oysters with the Parmesan cheese and then cover with the shrimp sauce. Broil until the top is bubbly - about 7 minutes.

This sauce is also great over broiled or baked fish!

Baked Catfish

1 pound catfish fillets
2 tablespoons no-sugar-
  added mayonnaise
1 teaspoon lemon juice
1/2 teaspoon creole
  mustard
1/4 teaspoon Worcester-
  shire sauce
1/4 teaspoon garlic powder
salt and pepper to taste
paprika

Rinse catfish fillets and pat dry. In a small bowl, combine the mayonnaise, lemon juice, mustard, Worcestershire sauce, garlic powder, salt, and pepper. Arrange the catfish in a greased casserole dish and spread the mayonnaise mixture over it. Sprinkle with paprika. Bake at 500F for fifteen minutes or until done.

Oysters Rockefeller

2 packages frozen spinach,
   cooked and drained
1 bunch green onions
1 stalk celery, strings
   removed
1 bunch parsley
1/2 teaspoon anise seed
   (optional)
1 sticks butter
1/2 cup bread crumbs from
   stone ground whole
   grain bread
3 tablespoons Worcester-
   shire sauce
1 tablespoon anchovy paste
salt, black pepper, red
   pepper to taste
1 1/2 pints oysters
Parmesan cheese

Grind the spinach, green onions, celery, parsley and anise seed in a meat grinder or food processor with the butter. Stir in the breadcrumbs, Worcestershire sauce, anchovy paste, salt, and pepper.

Place oysters on shells or ramekins and broil just until the edges start to curl. Drain the liquid from each shell. Cover with Rockefeller sauce and sprinkle with the Parmesan cheese. Place under the broiler until slightly brown.

Shrimp San Remo

1 pound raw shrimp, peeled
1/4 cup olive oil
1/4 stick butter
1 small can mushrooms,
   drained
1 cup chopped green
   onions
1 tablespoon stone ground
   whole grain flour
1/4 teaspoon salt
1/4 teaspoon garlic powder
cayenne pepper to taste
1 cup light sour cream

Melt the butter with the olive oil. In the mixture, sauté the shrimp until tender. Add drained mushrooms and green onions and cook for five more minutes. Stir in the flour, salt, garlic powder, and cayenne. Blend in the sour cream slowly. Cook for about ten minutes on low heat. This should be served hot, but do not let it boil after adding the sour cream.

Serve over stone ground whole grain pasta.

Seafood and Mushrooms in Wine Sauce

1 pound crab meat or
    shrimp
1/2 pound fresh mush-
    rooms, sliced
4 tablespoons butter
2 tablespoons stone ground
    whole grain flour
1/2 cup lowfat milk
1/2 cup white wine
1/4 teaspoon dry mustard
1/4 teaspoon tarragon
salt, pepper, & Tabasco
    to taste

Pick crab meat, carefully removing any shells but trying to leave the meat in lumps.

Clean mushrooms and dry well. Sauté the mushrooms and crab meat in three table-spoons of butter until the mushrooms are tender. Remove the mushrooms and crab meat from the pan with a slotted spoon, leaving the butter. Add flour to the butter and blend well. Add the milk slowly while blending. Then add the wine, mustard, tar-ragon, salt, pepper, and Tabasco. Cook for two or three minutes until sauce thickens. Stir constantly.

Place mushrooms and crabmeat in a cas-serole dish and pour the cream wine sauce over it. Dot with butter. Bake uncovered for 30 minutes at 350F.

This dish is really good with either crab-meat or shrimp; you can also use a combi-nation of the two.

Shrimp and Eggplant Casserole

2 large eggplants
1/4 cup olive oil
1 small bell pepper,chopped
1/2 cup chopped celery
1 medium onion, chopped
2 ripe tomatoes, peeled and
    chopped
1/2 tablespoon marjoram
salt and pepper to taste
cayenne pepper to taste
1 pound raw shrimp, peeled
    and chopped
1/4 cup crushed stone
    ground crackers
1/2 pound mozzarella
    cheese, shredded

Peel eggplant cut it into bite sized cubes. Boil the eggplant until tender and drain.

In a large pot, heat olive oil and sauté bell pepper, celery, and onion until tender. Add eggplant and sauté for another five minutes. Add tomatoes, marjoram, salt, and pepper and cook ten more minutes. Add shrimp and cook for another ten minutes.

Stir in the cracker crumbs and then pour into a casserole dish. Bake for thirty-five minutes at 350F.

Remove from the oven and distribute the mozzarella across the top. Return to the oven until the cheese melts.

Pan Trout

2 to 3 pounds of trout fillets
3 tablespoons butter
2 teaspoons minced garlic
1/2 cup white wine
3 tablespoons chopped
    green onions
2 tablespoons chopped
    parsley
salt and pepper to taste

Melt butter in a large skillet and sauté the garlic for several minutes. Season fish with salt and pepper and add to pan. Cook the fillets until almost done. Turn the fish and add the wine, green onions, and parsley. Cook until the fish flakes with a fork.

Shrimp Arnaud

2 pounds boiled shrimp,
  peeled
6 tablespoons olive oil
2 tablespoons tarragon
  vinegar
1 tablespoon paprika
1 tablespoon minced green
  onion
1 stalk celery, chopped
3 tablespoons horseradish
  mustard
1 tablespoon chopped
  parsley
1 tablespoon minced onion

Put all of the ingredients except the shrimp in a large bowl and mix well. Put the shrimp in the bowl and marinate for several hours. Serve the marinated shrimp with sauce on shredded lettuce.

New Orleans Remoulade Sauce

1 cup no-sugar-added
  mayonnaise
1 tablespoon minced onion
1/4 teaspoon minced garlic
1 tablespoon minced
  parsley
1 tablespoon minced celery
1 teaspoon horseradish
1 tablespoon tarragon
  vinegar
2 tablespoons Dijon
  mustard
1 teaspoon paprika
1 teaspoon Worcestershire
  sauce
1/4 cup salad oil
salt and Tabasco to taste

It is important to make this sauce the day before you use it so that the flavors have time to blend. Mix all ingredients in a bowl until well blended.

Note: For Shrimp Remoulade, top boiled shrimp with the sauce. Also great as a salad dressing!

108

A Little Different Remoulade

3 tablespoons horseradish
1/2 cup creole mustard
2 teaspoons crushed garlic
1 large onion, chopped
1/2 teaspoon celery salt
2 tablespoons paprika
2 tablespoons minced
   parsley
1 cup olive oil
2 tablespoons Worcester-
   shire sauce
2 boiled eggs, chopped
   fine
salt and pepper to taste

Combine all ingredients in a bowl and blend well.

Great with boiled shrimp and crawfish.

Celebrating Mardi Gras is something for which New Orleans is justifiably famous. Like most things in our area, it too has to do with food! In French, Mardi Gras means "fat Tuesday" and referred to the day before Ash Wednesday, when a fatted calf was the last meat meal before fasting and Lent began.

Shrimp Creole

1/2 cup stone ground whole grain flour
1/2 cup olive oil
1 cup chopped onion
1/2 cup chopped celery
1/4 cup chopped bell pepper
1/2 teaspoon chopped garlic
3 tablespoons chopped parsley
1/2 bunch chopped green onions
1/2 large cans tomatoes, chopped
1 small can no-sugar-added tomato paste
5 cups hot water
2 bay leaves
1 1/2 teaspoons salt
1/4 teaspoon cayenne pepper
1 dash black pepper
1 1/2 pounds raw peeled shrimp

Make a roux with the flour and olive oil at low heat. Add the chopped, onions, celery, bell pepper, and garlic. Cook these, stirring constantly, until tender. Add parsley and green onions and cook for another minute or two. Add tomatoes and tomato paste and blend in well. Stir in the hot water, bay leaves, salt, and pepper. Let simmer, uncovered, for one hour. Add cleaned, peeled shrimp and cook for another fifteen minutes. Serve over brown Basmati rice.

Trout Meuniere

6 large trout filets
stone ground whole grain
    flour
1 1/2 teaspoons salt
1/2 teaspoon pepper
6 tablespoons butter
2 tablespoons minced
    parsley
1 tablespoon lemon juice

Rinse trout filets and pat dry. Mix salt and pepper with the flour and roll fillets in the flour mixture. Melt the butter in a large frying pan and sauté the filets for five minutes. Turn the fish and sauté the other side for about four minutes. Put the trout on a warm serving dish and sprinkle with a little more salt and pepper. Add the lemon juice and the parsley to the butter remaining in the pan and heat until foamy. Pour over the trout and serve.

Variation: To turn Trout Meuniere into Trout Amandine, add slivered almonds to the butter, lemon, and parsley at the end. Pour the sauce over the trout.

Charcoal Grilled Whole Fish

Whole, cleaned trout, red
    snapper or mackerel
1/4 cup olive oil
juice of one lemon
1 tablespoon oregano
1 tablespoon tarragon
salt and pepper to taste

Heat charcoal until it is white hot.

In a bowl, mix the oil, lemon, oregano, tarragon, salt, and pepper. Rub the fish with the olive oil mixture and put it in a hinged basket grill.

Grill the fish about 4 inches from the coals. Cook about seven minutes on each side, basting while cooking.

Baked Fish Fillets St. Bernard

3 pounds of fish fillets such
    as bass, grouper,
    snapper, or drum
1/2 cup olive oil
2 large onions, chopped
1 can tomatoes with juice
1/2 cup white wine
1/2 cup chopped parsley
1/2 teaspoon minced garlic
salt and pepper to taste

In a large saucepan, sauté the onion in the olive oil until very tender. Add the tomatoes with juice, wine, parsley, garlic, salt and pepper. Stir well and simmer uncovered for fifteen minutes.

Place fish in a large casserole dish and cover with sauce. Bake at 350F for twenty-five minutes or until done.

Spicy Baked Shrimp

2 pounds large raw shrimp
1/3 cup butter
1 teaspoon salt
1 teaspoon black pepper
2 teaspoons minced garlic
1/4 cup chopped parsley
2 tablespoons lemon juice
2 teaspoons Worcestershire
    sauce

Peel shrimp leaving on the end section of the tail. Rinse and pat dry. Place in a large baking dish. Try to arrange all of the shrimp in one layer.

In a saucepan, heat the rest of the ingredients, melting the butter. Pour over the shrimp and bake at 400F for twenty minutes or until cooked. Turn shrimp over once during the cooking time and baste with sauce.

Casserole Grand Isle

1 can artichoke hearts
1 pound crabmeat
2 tablespoon olive oil
1/2 cup chopped onion
1 teaspoon minced garlic
1 pound peeled, raw shrimp
1/4 cup stone ground whole
    grain flour
3/4 cup chicken broth
2/3 cup evaporated skim
    milk
1 teaspoon dill
1/2 cup shredded cheddar
    cheese
salt and pepper to taste
Tabasco sauce to taste

Drain the artichokes well and squeeze out as much liquid as you can. Cut into quarters or smaller.

Pick through the crabmeat gently, making sure that all of the shells are removed.

In a large skillet, sauté the onion, garlic, and shrimp in the olive oil until the shrimp are done. Blend in the flour and then slowly pour in the chicken broth and milk while stirring to blend. Cook until the sauce begins to thicken. Add the dill, artichoke hearts, and cheese. Cook on low heat while gently folding in the crabmeat. Add salt, pepper, and Tabasco to taste.

Pour the mixture into a casserole dish and bake at 350F for 20 minutes.

Scampi and Fettuccini

2 tablespoons olive oil
1 bunch green onions,
    chopped
1 teaspoon minced garlic
1 tablespoon Worcester-
    shire sauce
2 pounds peeled raw
    shrimp
salt and pepper to taste
2 cups light sour cream

In a large skillet, sauté green onions and garlic in the olive oil until tender. Add the Worcestershire sauce, shrimp, salt, and pepper. Cook, stirring often, for about ten minutes.

Blend in the sour cream a little at a time, stirring to blend well. Do not allow the mixture to boil once you have added the sour cream. Serve over stone ground whole grain pasta.

Crawfish NaNa

1 pound crawfish tails
3 tablespoons olive oil
3 tablespoons butter
1 bunch green onions
    chopped
1/2 cup chopped parsley
3 tablespoons stone ground
    whole grain flour
1 can evaporated skim milk
2 tablespoons sherry
salt and cayenne to taste

In one skillet, sauté crawfish tails in the olive oil for about ten minutes.

In a larger skillet, sauté the green onions and parsley in the butter until tender. Blend in the flour. Add the milk gradually, stirring to blend. Cook this mixture on low heat until the sauce thickens. Add the sherry and the cooked crawfish tails.

You can serve this over stone ground whole grain pasta or as a dip.

Notes:

114

Aubergine with Crab

3 eggplants
1 ½ cups crabmeat
3 tablespoons butter
2 tablespoons stone ground
    whole grain flour
1 cup lowfat milk
2 teaspoons minced garlic
1 large onion, chopped
1 bell pepper, chopped
2 tablespoon chopped
    parsley
2 tablespoons olive oil
salt, pepper, and Tabasco
    to taste
paprika
Parmesan cheese

Cut eggplants in half lengthwise and put face down in a large greased baking dish. Cover with foil and bake at 350F for 40 minutes or until the eggplant is tender. Scoop out the pulp, leaving the shell for stuffing. Chop the pulp and set aside.

While the eggplant is baking, melt the butter in a small saucepan over low heat. Add the flour and blend well. Add the milk slowly while stirring. Cook on low heat until the sauce thickens. Remove from heat and stir in salt, pepper and Tabasco. Set aside.

In a skillet, sauté the garlic, onion, bell pepper, and parsley in the olive oil until translucent. Add the chopped eggplant pulp, salt, pepper, and Tabasco. Cook until well blended. Add the sauce that you prepared earlier and then fold in the crabmeat gently.

Sprinkle with paprika and Parmesan and bake at 425F for 15 minutes.

Variation: Substitute chopped boiled shrimp or crawfish.

Crawfish Stuffed Mushrooms

1 pound crawfish tails
2 dozen large fresh
    mushrooms
3 tablespoon olive oil
1/4 cup finely chopped
    onion
1/4 cup finely chopped bell
    pepper
1/4 cup finely chopped
    green onion
1 teaspoon finely chopped
    parsley
2 tablespoon stone ground
    whole grain flour
2 teaspoon dry mustard
3/4 cup low fat milk
salt and pepper to taste
1 teaspoon Worcestershire
    sauce
2 egg yolks
3 tablespoons olive oil
grated fresh Parmesan
    cheese

Rinse crawfish and drain. Chop into small pieces and set aside.

Clean mushrooms and pat dry. Remove the stems and chop them. In the olive oil, sauté the chopped stems with the onion, bell pepper, green onion, and parsley until they are tender. Sprinkle the flour and the dry mustard into this mixture and stir well. Add the crawfish and cook, stirring constantly for five minutes. Over lowered heat, stir milk in slowly, blending well. Add salt, pepper, and Worcestershire sauce.

In a cup, beat the egg yolks and then stir in a spoon or two of the hot milk mixture, blending well. Pour this into the crawfish and milk mixture and stir well. Let this cook for a minute or two. Remove the pot from the heat and allow to cool.

In a large skillet, sauté the mushroom caps in olive oil until tender but still firm. Stuff the caps with the crawfish mixture and place on a baking sheet. Sprinkle with Parmesan and bake in a preheated 450F oven until hot and puffy.

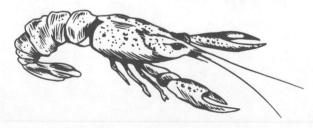

Sugarfree New Orleans
Poultry

Cajun Chicken

6 chicken breast halves
1 tablespoon red pepper
1 tablespoon black pepper
1 tablespoon paprika
2 tablespoons garlic
    powder
1 tablespoon oregano
1 tablespoon thyme
1 tablespoon onion powder
1 tablespoon salt
1/3 cup olive oil

Clean chicken, removing skin and all visible fat. Rinse with cold water and pat dry.

In a blender, mix red and black pepper, paprika, garlic powder, oregano, thyme, onion powder and salt. Slowly pour in the olive oil and blend until a thick paste is formed. Rub each chicken breast with the paste until it is thoroughly coated. Put the chicken on a greased broiler pan, cover, and refrigerate overnight so that the paste and seasonings can marinate the chicken.

Broil the chicken for fifteen minutes, turn and broil fifteen more. Cover pan with foil and bake at 300F for twenty more minutes.

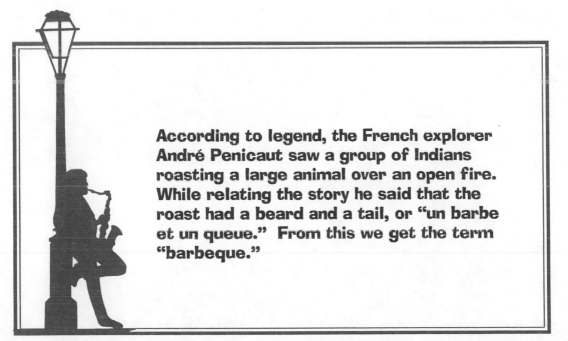

According to legend, the French explorer André Penicaut saw a group of Indians roasting a large animal over an open fire. While relating the story he said that the roast had a beard and a tail, or "un barbe et un queue." From this we get the term "barbeque."

French Quarter Chicken

2 whole chickens
3 tablespoons olive oil
juice of 1 lemon
2 teaspoons salt
1/2 cup olive oil
1 can tomatoes with juice
1 teaspoon pepper
1 tablespoon oregano
salt and cayenne to taste

Rinse chickens well and pat dry. Rub inside and out with three tablespoons of olive oil, lemon juice and salt. Bake at 375F for one hour.

In a saucepan, simmer the ½ cup of olive oil, tomatoes, pepper, oregano, salt and pepper for twenty minutes. Pour over the chicken and cook at 325F for an additional forty-five minutes, basting frequently.

Chicken Limone

2 chickens, in pieces
1/2 cup olive oil
juice of 2 lemons
1/4 cup oregano
salt and pepper to taste

Rinse chickens and pat dry. In a large bowl, combine the olive oil, lemon juice, oregano, salt, and pepper. Dip the chicken in the marinade one piece at a time, coating well. Put the chicken pieces in a large broiling pan and pour any remaining marinade over them. Marinate for at least four hours or overnight.

Broil the chicken about six inches from the heat with the fleshy side down for fifteen minutes. Turn the chicken pieces about half way through. Baste often while broiling.

Chicken with Green Peppercorn Sauce

4 boneless chicken breast
   halves, fat and skin
   removed
1 teaspoon olive oil
1/4 cup white wine
2 tablespoons onion –
   finely chopped
1/4 cup white wine
1/2 cup half and half
1 tablespoon green
   peppercorns
1/4 teaspoon dried tarragon

Preheat oven to 400F. In a large skillet sauté chicken breasts in olive oil until lightly browned on both sides. Place the chicken in a baking dish and bake for 15 minutes. Save the pan drippings in the sauté pan. While the chicken is baking, sauté onions in the skillet with the pan drippings until soft. Add wine, half-and-half, peppercorns, and tarragon. Heat until sauce coats the back of a spoon. Serve over baked chicken.

Chicken Breasts with Mushroom Crust

7 large boneless chicken
   breasts
2 tablespoons olive oil
3/4 pound fresh button
   mushrooms, sliced
3/4 pound fresh shitake
   mushrooms, sliced
1 bunch green onions,
   chopped
2 large garlic cloves,
   minced
1 teaspoon salt
1/2 teaspoon black pepper
1/4 stick chilled butter
   coarsely chopped

Clean chicken, removing skin and fat. In large heavy fry pan, heat olive oil over medium heat. Add mushrooms, green onions, and garlic; cook until lightly browned stirring occasionally. Remove from heat. Add salt and pepper. Cut up one chicken breast and place with butter in a food processor. Grind until smooth, pulsing processor on & off. Add mushroom mixture and chop coarsely, pulsing. Place chicken breasts between two sheets of wax paper and pound to even thickness. Divide mushroom/chicken mixture into 6 parts and carefully coat the six breasts. Place in parchment lined baking dish.

This can be prepared ahead and refrigerated. Bake in preheated 350F oven for 15 minutes. Serve whole or slice diagonally.

Chicken Cacciatore

4 pounds chicken pieces
   (with bone)
1/4 cup olive oil
Salt and cayenne to taste
2 medium onions, chopped
1/2 teaspoon minced garlic
1 bunch green onions,
   chopped
1/4 cup white wine
1 large jar no-sugar-added
   spaghetti sauce
2 bay leaves

Clean chicken, removing skin and fat. Salt and pepper the chicken and brown it in the olive oil in a large heavy pot. Remove the chicken and sauté the onions and garlic until tender. Put the chicken back in the pot and add the jar of spaghetti sauce. Simmer for 45 minutes. Add green onions, wine, and bay leaves; cover and cook for another twenty minutes.

Serve over stone ground whole grain pasta.

Chicken Carciofi

6 large chicken breasts
1 ½ teaspoons salt
1/2 teaspoon paprika
1/2 teaspoon cayenne
   pepper
6 tablespoons olive oil
1/2 pound fresh mush-
   rooms, cleaned and
   sliced
2 tablespoons stone ground
   whole grain flour
1 can chicken broth
1/2 cup white wine
1 can artichoke hearts
   well drained

Clean chicken breasts removing skin and fat. Sprinkle well with salt, paprika, and pepper. In a large skillet brown the chicken in four tablespoons of the olive oil. Remove the chicken to a large casserole dish. Add the rest of the olive oil to the skillet and sauté the sliced mushrooms until tender. Add the whole grain flour and stir to coat mushrooms. Stir in the broth and the wine. Simmer for five minutes.

Squeeze all liquid out of the artichoke hearts and cut in quarters. Place in the casserole dish around the chicken. Pour the mushroom sauce over the chicken and artichoke hearts and bake at 375F for forty minutes.

Chicken Divan

1 whole chicken, cut in
   pieces
1 package frozen broccoli
2 tablespoons stone ground
   whole grain flour
2 tablespoons olive oil
1 cup lowfat milk
1 tablespoon Worcester-
   shire sauce
1 cup grated cheddar
   cheese
1/4 cup Romano cheese

Cook broccoli according to directions on the package. Cut the broccoli into bite sized pieces and arrange in the bottom of a casserole dish.

Clean the chicken removing skin, all visible fat, and bones. (You may want to get boneless chicken breasts from your butcher instead!) Boil the chicken in salted water until cooked. Lay the chicken over the broccoli.

In a saucepan over medium heat, blend the olive oil and flour. Add the milk slowly while blending; add the Worcestershire sauce. Cook the sauce, stirring constantly until it thickens. Add the cheddar cheese and cook until it melts. Pour the cheese sauce over the chicken and broccoli and sprinkle with Romano cheese. Bake at 350F for fifteen minutes or until hot.

"Lagniappe" (lan-yap) is an old New Orleans expression meaning "a little something extra."

"Piquant" (pee-cont) means spicy and hot.

A "Roux" (roo) is the basis of many Creole and Cajun dishes. It is a blend of oil and flour cooked until brown, but never burnt!

Chicken in Wine Sauce

8 chicken breasts, no skin,
   no bones
1 stick butter
1/2 pound fresh mush-
   rooms, sliced
1 bunch green onions,
   sliced
2 tablespoons stone ground
   whole grain flour
1 teaspoon tomato paste
1 ½ cups canned chicken
   broth
1/2 cup red wine
salt and pepper to taste

In a frying pan, brown the chicken breasts well in the butter. Remove the chicken breasts from the pan and sauté the mushrooms and the onions. Stir in the flour, blending well. Add the tomato paste, broth, and wine. Bring to a boil and add salt and pepper.

Put the chicken breasts back in the pot, cover, and simmer until the chicken is tender - about 25 minutes.

Chicken Basting Sauce

1 teaspoon minced garlic
1/2 cup olive oil
2 tablespoons lemon juice
1 ½ tablespoons Worces-
   tershire sauce
1 tablespoon salt
1 teaspoon black pepper

Combine all of the ingredients. Using a pastry brush, baste chicken often while it is broiling. This sauce can also be used on baked chicken and on turkeys.

Chicken Lerici

1/2 pound fresh musrooms
8 whole chicken breasts
    without bones
8 thin slices lean ham
8 slices mozzarella cheese
salt and cayenne to taste
paprika
1/3 cup olive oil
3 tablespoons chopped
    green onions
2 cups light sour cream

Clean mushrooms and slice into thick slices. Set aside.

Clean chicken, removing skin and all fat. Pat dry. Slit breast lengthwise, but not all the way though, to form a pocket. Put the ham and the cheese inside the pocket. Season with salt and pepper. Roll the chicken up with the opening to the inside. Secure with a toothpick. Sprinkle each roll generously with paprika. Heat the olive oil in a heavy frying pan and brown the chicken rolls. Remove the chicken with a slotted spoon to a casserole dish.

In the remaining olive oil, saute the mushrooms and green onions for about five minutes on medium heat. Add sour cream and blend well. Pour the sour cream and mushroom mixture over the chicken. Cover tightly with foil and bake at 350F for 55 minutes or until done.

"Tasso" is a very highly seasoned Cajun version of smoked ham. When you can't find tasso, substitute Italian prosciutto.

"Andouille" (ahn-doo-ee) is a spicy Cajun pork sausage.

"Barbequed Shrimp" are peppery and delicious, but never barbequed!

Bourbon Street Chicken

4 chicken quarters
1/4 cup butter
1 teaspoon minced garlic
2 medium onion, sliced
4 cloves
2 bay leaf, broken in half
1 teaspoon salt
1 teaspoon coarsely ground
    pepper
2 cups white wine
1 cup light sour cream

In medium pan cook butter and garlic for about 2 minutes or until garlic is light brown. Add chicken and cook about 10 minutes or until the chicken is brown on all sides.

Place the onion slices on the bottom of the pan under the chicken; add cloves and bay leaf. Sprinkle the chicken with salt and pepper and pour in the wine. Cover, reduce temperature to low, and simmer about forty minutes or until a fork can be inserted in the chicken with ease.

Remove chicken to serving plates and keep warm. To the pan drippings, add sour cream and cook, stirring, about 2 minutes until warm but not boiling. Spoon over chicken.

Chicken Tchoupitoulas

3 pounds frying chicken,
    quartered
salt and cayenne to taste
1/3 cup olive oil
2 bunches green onions
    chopped
1/2 pound fresh mushrooms
    cleaned and sliced
1 carton light sour cream
1/4 cup white wine
1/2 cup hot water

Remove the skin and all visible fat from the chicken. Salt and pepper the chicken and brown in olive oil in a large heavy skillet. Remove the chicken to a platter. In the oil, sauté the green onions and mushrooms. Add sour cream slowly and blend well. Add the water and wine and stir to blend. Replace the chicken, cover and simmer for thirty minutes or until done.

Roasted Turkey Breast

1 turkey breast, 3 pounds
1 teaspoon minced garlic
1/2 teaspoon red pepper
1/2 teaspoon black pepper
1/2 teaspoon salt
2 tablespoons olive oil

Remove the skin and any visible fat from the turkey breast. Rinse and pat dry. In a bowl, combine the garlic, red pepper, black pepper, and salt. Rub the breast with the olive oil and then rub in the mixed seasonings. Place in a pan and add enough water to cover the bottom. Bake at 325F for one and a half hours or until done.

One of the best "doneness" tests for turkey is that the juices are totally clear when you puncture the meat with a sharp fork.

Turkey à la King

1/4 pound fresh mush-
 rooms, sliced
1/4 cup chopped onion
1/4 cup olive oil
1/4 cup stone ground whole
 grain flour
2 cups lowfat milk
1 teaspoon salt
1 1/2 cups cooked stone
 ground whole grain
 pasta
2 cups chopped cooked
 turkey meat
3/4 cup shredded Cheddar
 cheese
1 tablespoon Worcester-
 shire sauce
Tabasco to taste

In a large skillet, sauté the mushrooms and onion in the olive oil until tender. Stir in the flour and blend well. Add the milk a little at a time, stirring to blend. Cook until the sauce thickens.

Add all of the other ingredients and mix well. Turn into a greased casserole dish and bake, covered, for thirty minutes at 350F.

Crescent City Turkey and Oysters

1 tablespoon olive oil
2 teaspoons minced onion
1/2 pound mushrooms, sliced
1/2 stick butter
1/4 cup stone ground whole grain flour
1 teaspoon salt
1/2 teaspoon black pepper
1/4 teaspoon cayenne pepper
2 cups lowfat milk
1 egg yolk
2 tablespoons chopped parsley
1/4 teaspoon thyme
Tabasco to taste
1 pint oysters with liquid
2 cups chopped turkey meat

Don't even think of referring to this as leftover turkey. It's great!

Sauté onion and mushrooms in the olive oil until tender. Set aside.

In a large saucepan, melt the butter and blend in the flour. Add the salt, pepper, and cayenne. Add milk gradually while stirring. Allow to boil for one minutes, stirring constantly. Be careful not to scorch. Remove from heat.

In a cup, beat the egg yolk and spoon in a little of the hot milk mixture to blend. Pour the egg into the saucepan. Stir in parsley, thyme, and Tabasco.

In another saucepan, heat the oysters in their own juice until the edges begin to curl. Drain.

Add the oysters, onions, mushrooms, and turkey to the sauce in the large saucepan. Mix thoroughly.

Turn the entire mixture into a greased casserole dish and bake at 400F for about ten minutes or until the mixture is bubbly.

Herbed Turkey Cutlets

1/2 teaspoon basil
1/2 teaspoon tarragon
1/2 teaspoon thyme
1/2 teaspoon marjoram
1/2 teaspoon pepper
1/4 teaspoon salt
1 1/2 pounds of turkey
   breast, cut in 1/4"
   slices
1 tablespoon olive oil
1 1/2 teaspoon minced
   garlic
1 tablespoon stone ground
   whole grain flour
1/2 cup chicken broth
2 tablespoons lemon juice

Combine the basil, tarragon, thyme, marjoram, pepper, and salt. Sprinkle the mixture over both sides of the turkey cutlets. Heat the olive oil in a large skillet and sauté the garlic for a couple of minutes. Add the turkey and cook, browning well on both sides. Remove to a serving dish.

Add the flour to the pan and stir to blend with the drippings. Gradually add chicken broth and lemon juice, stirring constantly. Cook until the sauce thickens. Pour the sauce over the cutlets and serve.

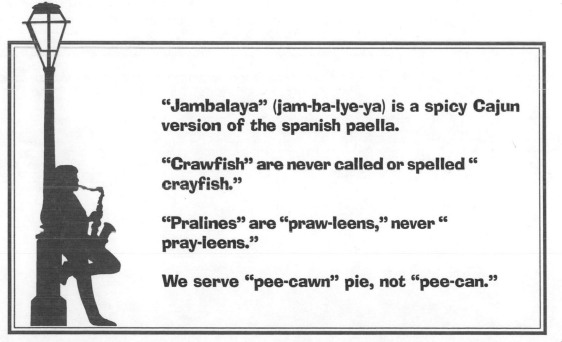

"Jambalaya" (jam-ba-lye-ya) is a spicy Cajun version of the spanish paella.

"Crawfish" are never called or spelled " crayfish."

"Pralines" are "praw-leens," never " pray-leens."

We serve "pee-cawn" pie, not "pee-can."

Sugarfree New Orleans
Meats

Beef Stroganoff

1 pound beef sirloin steak,
    cut in 1" strips
1/4 cup olive oil
1/2 teaspoon minced garlic
1/2 pound fresh mush-
    rooms, sliced
1 bunch green onions,
    chopped
1 teaspoon lemon juice
1/2 cup red wine
3/4 cup beef broth
salt and pepper to taste
1/4 pound stone ground
    whole grain noodles
1 cup light sour cream

In a skillet, sauté the garlic and mushrooms until tender. Add the beef and stir while browning. Add the green onions and stir. Stir in lemon juice, wine, broth, salt, and pepper. Simmer uncovered for fifteen minutes. Stir in the raw noodles; cover and cook for six minutes. Bite a noodle to see if it is done. Lower heat. Stir in sour cream slowly, blending well. You want to heat the sour cream, but don't let it boil. Serve immediately before noodles are overcooked.

Boeuf Vin Blanc

2 1/2 pounds boneless beef
    chuck, cut into
    1" pieces
olive oil
2 cups white wine
2 onions, sliced thin
6 tablespoons stone ground
    whole grain flour
2 cloves garlic, sliced thin
3 bay leaves
1 1/2 teaspoons salt
1 1/2 teaspoons thyme
1/4 teaspoon pepper
1 pound mushrooms, sliced
18 small white onions

Brown boneless beef chuck pieces (half at a time) in olive oil in ovenproof pot. Add wine, sliced onion, flour, garlic, bay leaves, salt, thyme and pepper. Stir gently. Cover and cook in 375F oven for 2 hours, stirring every half hour. Add mushrooms and onions; cover and continue cooking 2 hours, stirring occasionally. Adjust seasoning to taste. Remove bay leaves before serving.

Burgundy Beef

2 pounds lean beef roast,
    cut in 1" cubes
2 tablespoons olive oil
3 large onions, sliced
1 1/2 tablespoons stone
    ground whole grain
    flour
1 teaspoon marjoram
1/2 teaspoon thyme
salt and pepper to taste
1 cup beef broth
1 cup red wine
Tabasco sauce to taste
1/2 pound fresh mush-
    rooms, sliced

In a large heavy skillet sauté the onions in the olive oil until tender. With a slotted spoon, remove the onions to a dish. Toss the beef cubes in the flour, marjoram, thyme, salt, and pepper. Brown the beef cubes in the remaining olive oil - add a little more oil if necessary. Add 1/2 cup of the beef broth, wine, and Tabasco to the skillet. Simmer for two hours, stirring occasionally. If necessary, add a little more broth. Add the mushrooms and simmer for one more hour. The sauce should be thick and dark. You may need to add a little Kitchen Bouquet to correct the color.

Grillades

1 thick lean round steak
olive oil
Kitchen Bouquet
salt and pepper to taste
garlic powder to taste
olive oil
1 large onion, chopped fine
1/4 cup finely chopped
    celery
1/4 cup finely chopped bell
    pepper
1/3 cup finely chopped
    fresh parsley

Rub the steak with olive oil, Kitchen Bouquet, salt, pepper, and garlic powder. Pour enough olive oil in a large heavy skillet to cover the bottom. On high heat, brown the steak on both sides and remove to another dish. Lower the heat and sauté the onion, celery, bell pepper, and parsley. Put the steak back into the skillet and add two cups of hot water. Cover and allow to simmer for forty-five minutes or until tender. Remove the steak and let the gravy cook for a while uncovered to thicken.

Burgundy Beef Stew

1 pound lean boneless beef chuck, cut into 1 1/2" chunks

3 tablespoons stone ground whole grain flour

1 teaspoon salt

1/8 teaspoon pepper

1 tablespoon olive oil

1 large onions, cut in chunks

1/2 cup Burgundy wine

1 tablespoon tomato paste

1 teaspoon minced garlic,

1/4 teaspoon dried marjoram leaves, crushed

1/8 teaspoon dried thyme leaves, crushed

4 ounces mushrooms, halved

2 tablespoons fresh parsley, chopped

1 green pepper, cut in chunks

1 cup water

Trim fat from beef. Combine 2 tablespoons flour, salt and pepper. Coat the beef and brown in oil on stove. Add all other ingredients and stir to mix. Simmer for one hour or until tender.

And Then There's Meatloaf

1 medium onion, chopped
   fine
1/4 cup chopped bell
   pepper
1 tablespoon olive oil
2 pounds lean ground beef
2 eggs, beaten
1 1/2 teaspoons salt
1/4 cup chopped parsley
Pepper to taste
1 jar no-sugar-added
   spaghetti sauce

Sauté onion and bell pepper in the olive oil until tender. Put into a large bowl with the meat, egg, salt, parsley, and pepper. Blend very well with your cleaned hands. Roll the mixture into a loaf shape and put into a loaf pan. You should have a little room around all sides of the meat. Pour the spaghetti sauce over the meat loaf and bake at 350F for one and a half hours.

Beef San Gimignano

1 1/2 pounds round steak,
   cut 1/2 inch thick
salt and pepper to taste
1 egg, beaten
3/4 pound lean ground beef
1/2 cup grated fresh Parmesan cheese plus a little
1/3 cup chopped parsley
2 tablespoons olive oil
1 cup finely chopped onion
1/2 teaspoon minced garlic
1/2 cup red wine
1/4 cup no-sugar-added
   tomato sauce
1 can beef broth
1 teaspoon dried oregano

Pound steak with a kitchen mallet until the steak is 1/4" thick. Sprinkle with salt and pepper. In a bowl, mix the egg, ground beef, 1/2 cup Parmesan, parsley, salt, and pepper. Spread the mixture over the pounded steak. Roll up the steak and tie with string in several places. Heat the olive oil in a large skillet and brown the steak on all sides. Add the onion and garlic to the skillet and cook until the onion is soft. Add the wine and simmer for three minutes or until the wine is almost gone. Stir in the tomato sauce, broth, and oregano. Cover and cook on medium heat basting occasionally.

Serve with sauce on a bed of stone ground whole grain noodles.

Chili

4 pounds ground beef, extra
   lean
2 large onions, chopped
2 teaspoons minced garlic
2 cans tomatoes, chopped
2 tablespoons chili powder
2 teaspoons cumin powder
4 cans cooked red kidney
   beans, no sugar added
salt and pepper to taste
Tabasco sauce to taste

Spray your pot with vegetable oil spray or use olive oil if your ground beef is as lean as it should be. Brown the ground beef with the onions and garlic. Add the tomatoes, chili powder, and cumin and simmer uncovered for one hour. Add the drained beans and cook another 15 minutes. For a variation, you can serve into individual ovenproof bowls, topped with grated cheddar cheese.

Rump Roast Peking

lean rump roast
soy sauce
salt
garlic powder
black pepper
paprika
celery salt

Rub soy sauce into all sides of the roast. Rub in the salt, garlic, pepper, paprika, and celery salt. Bake uncovered at 400F for thirty minutes then lower the temperature to 250 and cook for three more hours or until done to your liking.

Marinated Eye of Round

1 lean eye of round roast
2 tablespoons olive oil
1/2 cup red wine
2 teaspoons minced garlic
1 /2 tablespoon pepper
salt to taste
1/3 cup lemon juice
1/3 cup Worcestershire
   sauce

To make the marinade, combine all of the ingredients except the roast and stir well. Put the roast in a large bowl and cover with marinade. Refrigerate for at least 24 hours, turning occasionally.

Roast uncovered, with marinade, for two hours or until done to your liking.

Moussaka

3 medium eggplants
2 medium onions,
    chopped fine
1/2 stick butter
1 1/2 pounds lean ground
    beef or ground lamb
salt and pepper
1/2 teaspoon thyme
2 small cans sugar free
    tomato paste
1/2 cup olive oil
3 eggs, separated
1 cup milk, lowfat
3 tablespoons chopped
    parsley
1 pound Swiss cheese,
    shredded
1/3 cup grated Parmesan
    cheese

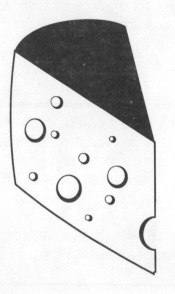

Slice the eggplants with rinds on (if tender) 1/4" thick. Put the slices to soak in a bowl of salted water for twenty minutes. This will remove the bitter taste that eggplant sometimes has.

In a large pan, sauté the onions in the butter until tender. Add the beef and cook until it browns. Add salt, pepper, thyme, and tomato paste. Remove from heat. Taste for seasoning and correct if necessary.

Drain the eggplant and pat dry. In a different large pan, heat the olive oil and sauté the eggplant slices until they turn golden in color. Place half of the eggplant in the bottom of a large greased casserole dish.

Beat the egg whites until they are stiff and fold them into the meat mixture. Pour half of this into the casserole over the eggplant.

Beat the egg yolk into the milk with a fork. Add the parsley and Swiss cheese. Pour half of this over the eggplant and meat. Repeat with layers of eggplant, meat sauce, and cheese sauce. Top with Parmesan cheese and bake at 350F for 35 minutes.

NaNa's Lasagna

1 1/2 pounds lean ground
    beef
1/2 cup chopped green
    onions
1 jar no sugar added
    spaghetti sauce
1 cup creamed cottage
    cheese
1 cup light sour cream
12 ounces stone ground
    whole grain noodles,
    cooked
1 teaspoon olive oil
salt
1 cup shredded cheddar
    cheese

Cook the noodles according to directions with a little olive oil and salt. Drain and set aside.

In a hot skillet, brown the ground meat. Add onions and sauce and cook for five minutes. In a large bowl, combine the cottage cheese and sour cream and then add the noodles. Stir well. Put half of the noodle mixture into a casserole dish. Spoon half of the meat sauce over this. Repeat this process and then top with the cheddar cheese. Bake in a preheated 350F oven for 30 minutes.

This is a great dish to prepare ahead and then pop into the oven when your guests arrive.

Marinated Roast Beef

lean roasting beef of your
    choice
1/2 cup olive oil
1/2 cup soy sauce
1/4 cup Worcestershire
    sauce
1/4 cup lemon juice
1 large onion, sliced
salt and pepper to taste

Mix the olive oil, soy sauce, Worcestershire sauce, and lemon juice together. Put the roast in a bowl. Rub the marinade into the meat and put the excess into the bowl with the beef and the onions. Refrigerate for at least three hours, turning the roast several times. Bake in a 350F oven for forty-five minutes or until done, basting often. The timing will depend on the cut and the size of your roast.

Rosita's Greek Hamburger

3 large onions, sliced thin
2 tablespoons olive oil
1 pound ground beef, extra
    lean
1 egg, beaten
1 small onion, chopped fine
salt and pepper
1/4 pound Feta cheese,
    crumbled
6 pieces stone ground
    whole grain pita bread

Sauté onions in olive oil until they are browned. Sprinkle with salt and pepper while they are cooking. Remove with a slotted spoon to another dish.

Mix ground meat with egg, onion, salt, and pepper and shape into six patties. Fry in a skillet until almost done. Put crumbled Feta cheese on each pattie; put a lid on the skillet and cook for two minutes.

On each plate, put a piece of pita bread, a hamburger pattie with Feta and cover with onion rings.

Spaghetti Meat Sauce

1 pound extra lean ground
    beef
1 large onion, chopped
2 teaspoons minced garlic
1/2 cup olive oil
2 cans no-sugar-added
    tomato sauce,
    (8 oz. each)
2 cans no-sugar-added
    tomato paste
    (6 oz. each)
1 tablespoon Worcester-
    shire sauce
1/4 cup chopped parsley
1/2 pound fresh mushrooms
    cleaned & quartered
salt and cayenne to taste
Tabasco sauce to taste

Sauté the beef, onion, and garlic in olive oil until the beef is browned. Add tomato sauce and paste, Worcestershire sauce, parsley, mushrooms, salt and pepper, and Tabasco. Simmer uncovered for two and a half hours stirring occasionally.

Add a little hot water if the sauce becomes too thick. Serve over stone ground whole grain pasta.

Pasta Carbonara

1 1/2 pounds stone ground
    whole grain noodles
1 1/2 tablespoons olive oil
1/2 pound prosciutto, diced
1/4 cup chopped parsley
1 teaspoon minced onion
1 cup light cream
1/4 pound Parmesan cheese
3 egg yolks, beaten
salt and pepper to taste

Cook the noodles according to directions while you are preparing the sauce.

Sauté the prosciutto in hot olive oil until the prosciutto is crispy. Remove from pan with a slotted spoon. In the remaining oil, sauté the parsley and onion. Add the cream and heat until warm, but do not boil. Remove from heat and stir in the beaten egg yolks. Pour this mixture over the drained noodles. Toss with Parmesan, salt, and pepper. Serve hot.

Pasta Pie

6 ounces stone ground
    whole grain pasta
3 tablespoons olive oil
1/3 cup grated fresh
    Parmesan cheese
2 eggs, well beaten
1 cup ricotta cheese
1/2 cup chopped onions
1/4 cup bell pepper
1/2 teaspoon minced garlic
1 pound lean ground beef
1 small can no-sugar-added
    tomato paste

Cook pasta according to package directions and drain well. Stir half of the olive oil into the hot pasta; stir in the Parmesan and eggs. Put the pasta into a well-greased pie pan. Form the pasta into a firm "pie crust" covering the sides and bottom of the dish. Spread the ricotta cheese over the pasta crust.

Put the remaining olive oil into a skillet and sauté the onions, bell pepper, and garlic. Add ground meat and brown. Drain off any excess grease. Stir in tomatoes, tomato paste and oregano, and simmer 10 minutes. Spoon the meat sauce over the ricotta layer. Bake the pie in a preheated 350F oven for twenty minutes. Sprinkle the shredded mozzarella on top of the pie and bake until the cheese melts.

Sugar Busting Lasagna

1/2 cup olive oil
1 large onion, chopped
1 teaspoon minced garlic
1 1/2 pounds ground beef,
    extra lean
1/4 teaspoon oregano
salt and cayenne to taste
1 can no-sugar-added
    tomato paste
1 cup hot water
1/2 pound stone ground
    whole grain noodles
1 teaspoon salt
1 tablespoon olive oil
1/2 pound mozzarella
    cheese, shredded
1 pint ricotta cheese
1/2 cup grated Romano
    cheese

In a large skillet sauté the onion and garlic in the olive oil until the onion is tender. Add the ground beef and brown. Add the oregano, salt, pepper, tomato paste and hot water. Stir to blend. Simmer, stirring occasionally, over low heat for about an hour.

Cook the noodles as directed with salt and olive oil. Drain well. In a casserole dish, layer meat sauce, mozzarella, ricotta, noodles and then repeat. Spoon the last of the meat sauce on the top layer of noodles. Sprinkle the Romano over the meat sauce and bake at 375F for 30 minutes.

Spicy Beef Sandwiches

8 ounces beef round steaks,
    cut into 1/4" strips
2 teaspoons vegetable oil
1 medium onion, sliced
1 medium jalapeno pepper,
    cut into rings
1/8 teaspoon crushed garlic
salt to taste
2 stone ground, whole grain
    pita breads
1/4 cup chopped tomato

On medium-high heat sauté onion, jalapeno pepper and garlic in oil for 3 to 4 minutes or until lightly browned. Remove from skillet. Add beef strips to the skillet and cook 1 to 2 minutes, turning once. Do not overcook. Season with salt and pepper. Place beef on roll. Top with onion mixture and chopped tomatoes.

144

Together Tacos

2 pounds lean ground beef
4 tablespoons olive oil
1 large onion
1 medium bell pepper
1/2 cup chopped celery
1 teaspoon minced garlic
3 tablespoons chili powder
salt and cayenne to taste
2 cans no-sugar-added
    tomato sauce
2 cans red kidney beans
1 1/2 cups hot water
Triscuits, chopped coarsely
1/2 pound cheddar cheese,
    shredded

In a large heavy pot, sauté onions, bell peppers, celery, and garlic in olive oil until tender. Add the ground beef and brown well. Add chili powder, salt, and cayenne and stir. Stir in the tomato sauce, beans, and hot water. Simmer uncovered for 50 minutes, stirring occasionally.

The chili should be quite thick at the end of the cooking time. If it thickens too early in the process, stir in a little hot water.

Pour into a large serving bowl or individual dishes. Top with chopped Triscuits and shredded cheese.

Sirloin au Vin

2 pound sirloin steak, very
    lean, cut 3/4" thick
1 tablespoon olive oil
1/2 pound sliced fresh
    mushrooms
1/2 cup chopped green
    onions
3/4 cup red wine
3/4 cup canned beef broth
2 tablespoons no-sugar-
    added tomato paste
1 teaspoon tarragon
2 tablespoons chopped
    parsley

In a large skillet, brown the steak in the olive oil. Add the mushrooms and green onions and cook until tender. (If your skillet is not large enough, you may have to do the mushrooms first and then remove them while you brown the steak.)

Add the wine, beef broth, tomato paste, tarragon, and parsley. Bring to a boil and then simmer for ten minutes or until the steak is done to your liking.

Steak Costa del Sol

2 round steaks, very lean
   1 1/2 pounds each, cut
   3/4" thick
8 ounces light cream
   cheese, softened
1/2 cup slivered almonds
1/2 cup grated onion
1/2 cup sliced green olives
1/2 cup sliced ripe olives
salt and pepper to taste
olive oil
1 cup hot water

Stir almonds, onion, and olives into the softened cream cheese, blending well. Set aside.

On a board, with a kitchen mallet, pound steaks out thin. Sprinkle with salt and pepper. Spread the cream cheese mixture evenly on each steak. Roll each steak up and tie with string. Brown on all sides in olive oil.

Place the steaks in a roasting pan with the hot water. Cover the pan and bake at 350F for about two hours or until tender.

Pepper Cubed Steaks

4 beef cubed steaks
Kitchen Bouquet
1 1/2 teaspoons black
   pepper, coarse ground
salt to taste
3 tablespoons olive oil
1/3 cup water
1 teaspoon lemon juice
1 teaspoon Worcestershire
   sauce

Rub the steaks with Kitchen Bouquet and then sprinkle with pepper and salt and press in. In a large skillet, brown the meat well on both sides in the olive oil. Cubed steaks do not take long to cook. Remove the steaks to a platter and keep warm.

Stir the water, lemon juice, and Worcestershire sauce into the pan drippings, stir well and cook down a little. Pour the sauce over the steaks and serve.

Island Barbeque Sauce

1 can whole tomatoes
1 onion finely chopped
2/3 cup olive oil
1 teaspoon minced garlic
1/4 cup lime juice
dash of dried basil
salt and pepper to taste
Tabasco sauce to taste

Drain the tomatoes and chop as finely as you can. Put the tomatoes and onions in a saucepan and simmer uncovered for fifteen minutes. Mash the tomatoes or put into the blender. Add the olive oil, garlic, lime, basil, salt, pepper, and Tabasco to the tomato puree and simmer uncovered for about an hour. Use this sauce to baste meat while grilling

Ground Meat and Cabbage Casserole

1 head cabbage
1 pound very lean ground meat
1 medium onion, chopped
1/2 teaspoon minced garlic
olive oil
16 ounce can of no sugar added tomato sauce
1 teaspoon salt
1/4 teaspoon thyme
1/2 teaspoon pepper
Parmesan cheese, grated

Rinse cabbage and tear into pieces. Set aside to drain.

Sauté the meat, onion, and garlic in olive oil. Drain off any grease. Add tomato sauce, salt, thyme, and pepper. Stir to blend and add salt if needed.

In a greased casserole, place half of the cabbage, and then half of the meat sauce. Repeat the layers and then top with Parmesan cheese. Bake at 350F for 45 minutes.

147

Pepper Veal Steaks

veal round steaks, cut
    about 1/2 inch thick
1/4 cup stone ground whole
    grain flour
1 teaspoon paprika
1/2 teaspoon garlic powder
1/2 teaspoon basil
1/2 teaspoon oregano
2 tablespoons olive oil
1/2 cup white wine
1/2 cup chicken broth
2 large bell peppers
1/2 pound sliced fresh
    mushrooms
1 tablespoon lemon juice
2 tablespoons chopped
    green onion

In a bowl, mix the flour, paprika, garlic powder, basil, and oregano well. Dredge the veal through this mixture. On a board, with a kitchen mallet, pound the veal out to 1/4 inch thickness. In a skillet, brown the veal well on both sides in the olive oil. When the veal is done to your liking, move it into a serving dish.

Add the wine, chicken broth, peppers, mushrooms, lemon juice, and green onion to the pan with the veal drippings. Cook until the peppers and mushrooms are tender. Put the veal back in the pan long enough to heat it before serving.

In New Orleans, when someone says, "Today's Monday" what they usually mean is that it's time for red beans and rice! Traditionally, Monday was wash day in the old Creole or Cajun household. Since this was a tedious chore, the cook could put the pot of beans on the stove to simmer unattended while she spent her day doing laundry.

Most New Orleans restaurants still serve red beans on Mondays.

Yes, You Can Have Pizza!

3 whole grain pita breads
1 tablespoon olive oil
1 teaspoon minced garlic
6 slices Canadian bacon,
    cut into bite size
2 cups mozzarella cheese
    shredded

Preheat oven to 425F. With a sharp knife, carefully slice through the edge of the pita bread so that you can split each one into two rounds. Drizzle each one with olive oil and garlic. Distribute the Canadian bacon evenly and then top each pizza with cheese. Bake for five minutes.

Note: *I bought a jar of minced garlic in the grocery store and drained the water that the garlic was packed in. I replaced it with olive oil. This is the oil I use for pizzas and in many other dishes. When the oil level gets low, I just add more.*

Pizza variations: No-sugar-added tomato sauce, ripe olives, sun dried tomatoes, thin sliced onions, chopped artichoke hearts, spinach (make sure these last two are drained and dried), cooked or canned mushrooms, bell peppers, pine nuts, and different types of cheese. Be adventurous, almost anything works!

Barbequed Pork Chops

lean pork chops, 3/4 inch
    thick
olive oil
Kitchen Bouquet
salt and pepper to taste
lemon pepper
oregano

Carefully trim all fat from the pork chops. Rub each one with olive oil and a little Kitchen Bouquet. Sprinkle each with salt, pepper, lemon pepper, and a little oregano. Press the seasonings into the meat. Place on the barbeque grill and cook, turning once, for 25 minutes or until the pork is no longer pink.

Pork Chops Piquant

4 lean pork loin chops, cut
    1 inch thick
1/4 teaspoon Kitchen
    Bouquet
1 tablespoon olive oil
salt and pepper to taste
1/2 cup chicken broth
1/4 cup white wine
1 bell pepper, chopped
1 medium onion, chopped

Trim all fat from the pork chops. Rub the Kitchen Bouquet into the chops and then brown in the olive oil. Sprinkle with salt and pepper. Add broth and wine and simmer covered for 30 minutes. Add the bell pepper and onion and cook uncovered until the pepper is tender.

Grilled Pork Tenderloin

2 very lean pork tenderloins
    1 pound each
3 tablespoons olive oil
2 teaspoons chopped
    rosemary
1 teaspoon minced garlic
salt and pepper to taste

Trim any visible fat from the tenderloins and place in a shallow ovenproof dish.

Combine the olive oil, rosemary, garlic, salt, and pepper in a small bowl. Rub this marinade into the tenderloins and refrigerate for at least 2 hours. Bake at 350F until well done or cook on an open grill.

Pork Chops Amalfi

4 very thick, very lean pork
    chops
salt and pepper to taste
1 onion, sliced thin
1 lemon, sliced
1 bell pepper, sliced
2 cups no-sugar-added
    tomato juice

In a hot skillet, brown chops well on both sides. Add salt and pepper, onion, lemon, and bell pepper slices. Add the tomato juice and simmer uncovered for one hour.

Garlic Leg of Lamb

3 pounds leg of lamb
3 cloves garlic, slivered
olive oil
salt and pepper
white wine

Carefully trim the lamb of all fat. With a sharp knife make slits deep into the lamb and slide in slivers of garlic. Sprinkle the lamb generously with olive oil, salt, and pepper. Place in a heavy roasting pan and cook at 425F for 45 minutes or until done. Remove the lamb to a serving dish.

Carefully remove the grease from the meat drippings. Pour the meat drippings, scraping the pan, into a small sauce pan. Dilute with a little white wine and simmer for five minutes.

Burgundy Lamb Chops

4 lamb chops, cut 1 1/2
    inches thick
1/4 cup burgundy wine
3 tablespoons olive oil
1/3 cup chopped onion
1/8 teaspoon minced garlic
1/4 teaspoon cumin
salt and pepper to taste

In a small bowl, mix the wine, oil, onion, garlic, cumin, salt, and pepper.

Trim the lamb chops of all fat and place in a shallow glass baking pan. Stir the marinade again and pour over the chops. Refrigerate for at least two hours, turning chops several times.

Remove the chops from the marinade and place on a broiler pan. Broil 3 to 5 inches from the heat for about twenty minutes or until done to your liking. Baste occasionally with the marinade. The chops can also be cooked on an outdoor grill.

Lamb en Brochette

4 pounds leg of lamb
    boned and trimmed
1/2 pound bacon
    thick-sliced
1 pound fresh mushrooms
2 tablespoons lemon juice
3 cloves garlic, minced
1 teaspoon salt
1 teaspoon black pepper
1/2 cup olive oil
skewers

Cook bacon in simmering water for 5 minutes to defat. Drain, pat dry and cut into two inch pieces. Wrap and refrigerate.

Clean mushrooms, patting dry and removing stems. Cut lamb into 1 1/2" cubes.

In a medium bowl, blend lemon juice, garlic, salt, pepper, and olive oil. Add lamb cubes and mushrooms tossing until they are well coated. Cover this mixture and allow to marinate for 6 to 24 hours.

Preheat oven to 475F. Alternate lamb, bacon, and mushrooms on skewers and arrange on baking sheet. Cook until the lamb is browned outside but still pink inside, approximately fifteen minutes.

Note: *If you are using wooden skewers, soak them in water for at least twenty minutes before using. This will keep them from burning.*

Sugarfree New Orleans
Desserts

YumYum Chocolate Sauce

3/4 cup unsweetened cocoa
1 cup lowfat milk
2 tablespoons butter
2 teaspoons vanilla extract
sugar substitute to taste

In a small saucepan stir milk slowly into the cocoa, stirring until blended. Add butter and cook over medium heat until the mixture starts to thicken. Remove from heat and stir in vanilla and sugar substitute. If the sauce is not totally smooth, put it in the blender for 1 minute. If it needs to be thinned, add a little milk. Refrigerate.

Serve over "no sugar added" ice cream.

Voodoo Chocolate Sauce

3 squares unsweetened
  baking chocolate
12 ounces skim evaporated
  milk
4 tablespoons butter
2 teaspoons vanilla
sugar substitute to taste

In a small saucepan, melt the chocolate squares in the evaporated milk and butter. Stirring constantly, simmer the sauce until it thickens. Remove from heat and stir in the vanilla and sugar substitute.

Cola Jello

2 packages sugar free
  raspberry jello
1 1/2 cups boiling water
1 20 ounce bottle diet cola,
  very cold
1 cup chopped pecans,
1 package cream cheese
  very cold

Add the boiling water to the jello. Stir until dissolved. Allow to cool for 10 minutes. Stir in the cold cola and nuts. Refrigerate until congealed. When it is time to serve, grate frozen cream cheese over the jello.

Raspberry Mousse

1 pound frozen raspberries
1 pint light cream
1 envelope gelatin

Thaw the frozen raspberries and mash with a fork saving a few whole ones for decoration.

In a bowl, whip the cream with the gelatin until the cream is stiff. Fold in the raspberries. Spoon into individual serving dishes and garnish with the remaining raspberries. Refrigerate for several hours before serving.

Crumb Pie Crust

1 1/2 cup fine crushed low
    sodium stone ground
    crackers
3 tablespoons soft butter
1 tablespoon water
2 packets sugar substitute

Combine crumbs with butter and water. Add sugar substitute. Spread the dough in a pie pan, pressing firmly into the sides and bottom.

This crust can be used chilled as is or it can be baked if necessary.

Strawberries with Dip

Fresh strawberries with
    Stems on
light sour cream
brown sugar substitute
    to taste

Mix sour cream with sugar substitute in a small dip bowl. Surround with cleaned fresh strawberries. Dip the strawberries into the sour cream mixture and enjoy!

Lemon Blueberry Pie

3 eggs
1/3 cup evaporated skim
    milk
1 teaspoon lemon extract
1/2 cup "fruit only" blue-
    berry jam
1 packet unflavored gelatin
1/4 cup water
dash of salt
3 cups fresh blueberries
    rinsed and drained

Beat the eggs, milk, and lemon extract together until smooth. Pour into a crumb pie shell and bake at 350 for 10 minutes.

In a saucepan, sprinkle the gelatin over the water and let stand for one full minute. Add the blueberry jam and salt and stir to dissolve the gelatin. Bring the mixture to a boil, stirring constantly. Fold in the blueberries. Allow to cool for a couple of minutes and then spread over the custard in the pie plate. Chill until firm.

Cheesecake

1 package cream cheese,
    8 ounces, softened
2 tablespoons lemon juice
1 egg separated
2 tablespoons sugar
    substitute or to taste
2/3 cup skim milk
1 packet unflavored gelatin
2 tablespoon water
1 crumb pie crust

Beat the cream cheese with the lemon juice until smooth. In a saucepan, heat the egg yolk, sweetener, and milk on low heat until it is thick enough to coat a spoon, but be careful not to boil. Remove from heat and slowly stir thoroughly into the cream cheese mixture.

In a cup, sprinkle the gelatin over the water. Let stand for a full minute. Microwave on high for 40 seconds and then stir thoroughly. Blend this mixture into the cream cheese.

Beat the egg white until stiff and then fold it into the cream cheese. Pour this filling into the pie crust. And chill until set.

Spiced Blueberry Sauce

2 cups blueberries
2 teaspoons grated orange
    rind
2 teaspoons grated lemon
    rind
1/2 teaspoon ground
    cinnamon
1/2 teaspoon allspice
1/2 cup water
sugar substitute to taste

In a microwavable bowl, combine all ingredients except the sugar substitute. Microwave on high for two minutes. Stir the mixture and then microwave for two more minutes until the berries are tender and the sauce is bubbling. Remove from heat and stir in the sugar substitute. Great over no-sugar-added vanilla ice cream or custard.

Peaches and Cream

4 ripe peaches, peeled and
    sliced
1 cup water
1/3 cup cream cheese,
    softened
1 1/2 teaspoons brown
    sugar substitute
2 packets unflavored gelatin
1/2 cup evaporated skim
    milk

In a large saucepan, cook the peaches, water, and cream cheese over medium heat for five minutes. Stir in sugar substitute.

In a cup, sprinkle the gelatin over the milk and let stand for one full minute and then mix well to dissolve.

Remove the peach mixture from the heat and stir in the milk, mixing well. Pour into individual dishes and refrigerate for several hours or until firm. Serve chilled.

Raspberry Bavarian

1 small package no sugar
    raspberry gelatin
1 cup plain yogurt
1 teaspoon vanilla extract
2 large egg whites
3 packets sugar substitute
1 cup fresh raspberries

In a bowl, combine gelatin with 1 cup of boiling water. Stir until dissolved. When cooled, stir in yogurt and vanilla and chilled until thickened. Stir occasionally while the mixture is thickening.

In another bowl, beat egg white and sugar substitute until soft peaks form when the beaters are lifted. Fold the egg whites and half of the fresh raspberries into the gelatin mixture and refrigerate. Top each serving with some of the remaining raspberries.

Broiled Apple Rings

4 small apples
1 packet sugar substitute
1/2 teaspoon ground
    cinnamon

Wash apples and slice into 1/2 inch rounds. Using a cookie cutter or sharp knife, core each slice.

In a cup, combine the sugar substitute and cinnamon.

Place rings on a greased cookie sheet and broil for 8 minutes or until light browned. With a spatula, gently turn each ring. Sprinkle the rings with the cinnamon mixture and broil for one more minute. These are good hot or cold.

Key Lime Pie

1 packet unflavored gelatin
3 tablespoons fresh lime
  juice
1/2 cup boiling water
9 packets sugar substitute
  or to taste
1 cup evaporated skim milk
1 teaspoon vanilla
juice of 1 1/2 more fresh
  limes
2 drops green food coloring
1 crumb pie crust

Sprinkle the gelatin over the lime juice and allow to stand for one full minute. Add the boiling water and stir to dissolve the gelatin. Add the sweetener and stir well. Refrigerate until slightly thickened, about 45 minutes.

Meanwhile, combine milk and vanilla and freeze for thirty minutes. Remove this from the freezer and beat with an electric mixer at high speed until the milk is stiff. Slowly stir in the rest of the lime juice and the food coloring. Blend in the gelatin mixture carefully.

Pour the filling into the pie crust and chill until firm.

Whipped Topping

1/2 cup instant dry milk
1/2 cup cold water
2 teaspoons lemon juice
1/2 teaspoon vanilla
sugar substitute to taste

Mix the dry milk and water well and refrigerate of thirty minutes. Beat at high speed for four minutes. Add lemon juice and beat for four more minutes while stirring in the vanilla and sugar substitute. Refrigerate.

"No sugar added" ice creams are a real boon to the Glycemic Index dieter and they are available at every grocery store. They can be used in a variety of ways.

The Old Fashioned Purple Cow

Vanilla no-sugar-added ice
    cream
Diet root beer

Scoop vanilla ice cream into a glass and top off with diet root beer.

It's like being a kid again!

Italian Bisque Tortoni

1/2 gallon no-sugar-added
    vanilla ice cream
3/4 cup slivered almonds
    toasted and chopped
2 tablespoons almond
    extract
1 cup blueberries
1 cup coarsely crushed
    triscuits

Let the ice cream soften until it is soft enough to stir, but not melted. Stir in the almonds, almond extract, blueberries, and Triscuits. Put mixture back in freezer to set up.

Strawberry Parfait

Strawberries, cleaned,
    hulled, and sliced
sugar substitute to taste
1 recipe Okay Whipped
    Topping
Vanilla no-sugar-added Ice
    cream

Sprinkle strawberry slices with sweetener and toss to coat. Fold strawberries into the Okay Whipped Topping and refrigerate. Serve the ice cream into parfait glasses and top with the strawberry mixture.

Lemon & Blue Berry Ice Cream Pie

1 quart no-sugar-added
    vanilla ice cream
lemon extract to taste
2/3 cup "fruit only" blue-
    berry jam
1 packet unflavored gelatin
dash of salt
1 cup fresh blueberries
    rinsed and drained
1 crumb pie crust

Thaw ice cream enough so that it can be stirred. Stir in the lemon extract. Press the ice cream into the pie shell and freeze until firm.

In a saucepan, sprinkle the gelatin over the water and let stand for one full minute. Add the blueberry jam and salt and stir to dissolve the gelatin. Bring the mixture to a boil, stirring constantly. Fold in the blueberries. Allow to cool. Spread over the ice cream when it is time to serve.

Vanilla & Peanut Butter Ice Cream Pie

1 quart no-sugar-added
    vanilla ice cream
1 teaspoon unflavored
    gelatin
2/3 cup no-sugar-added
    crunchy peanut butter
1/2 cup low fat milk
2 packets sugar substitute
1 crumb pie crust

Thaw ice cream enough so that it can be stirred. Press it into the pie shell and freeze until firm.

Sprinkle gelatin over 1/4 cup of the milk and set aside.

In a double boiler, melt the peanut butter with the remaining milk, stirring constantly until smooth. Add the soaked gelatin and cook, stirring until the gelatin is completely dissolved. Remove from heat and stir in the sweetener.

Spread this mixture over the ice cream and then drizzle with sugar free chocolate sauce. Place in the freezer until a little before serving time

Grasshopper Pie

1 quart no-sugar-added
   chocolate ice cream
2 teaspoons unsweetened
   cocoa
1 quart no-sugar-added
   vanilla ice cream
1/2 teaspoon mint extract
sugar free chocolate sauce
1 crumb pie crust

Stir the cocoa into the chocolate ice cream that has been softened just to the point that it can be stirred. Blend well and pack into the pie crust. Freeze until firm.

Stir the mint extract into the softened vanilla ice cream. Pack the mixture over the chocolate ice cream and drizzle with chocolate sauce. Freeze until firm.

Allow the pie to soften a little before serving.

Dreaming up your own combinations is fun. Try vanilla ice cream and baked apples or chocolate and mocha (use a little instant coffee powder in vanilla ice cream).

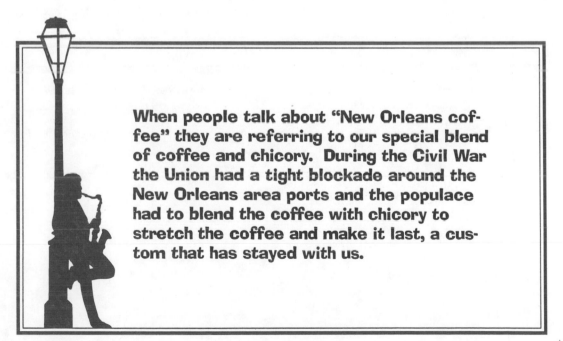

When people talk about "New Orleans coffee" they are referring to our special blend of coffee and chicory. During the Civil War the Union had a tight blockade around the New Orleans area ports and the populace had to blend the coffee with chicory to stretch the coffee and make it last, a custom that has stayed with us.

INDEX OF RECIPES

Sugarfree New Orleans

P.O. Box 750855, New Orleans, LA 70175
Telephone: Toll-free: 1 (888) 607-4002
In New Orleans, call (504) 269-3463
www.toutsuite.com

Please send _____ copies of Sugarfree New Orleans at $15.95 plus $2.50 postage and handling. Louisiana residents add 4% sales tax ($0.64 per book purchased).

_____ Check if gift wrap is desired . *(Please add $1.50 per copy gift wrapped.)*

_____ Enclosed is my check or money order for $_____.
Make check payable to Sugarfree New Orleans.

_____ Charge to ___ VISA ____Mastercard ____AmEx

Card No._____

Exp. Date_____ Name on Card _____

Signature_____

Name_____

Address_____

City_____ State_____ ZIP_____

Telephone_____

Sugarfree New Orleans

P.O. Box 750855, New Orleans, LA 70175
Telephone: Toll-free: 1 (888) 607-4002
In New Orleans, call (504) 269-3463
www.toutsuite.com

Please send _____ copies of Sugarfree New Orleans at $15.95 plus $2.50 postage and handling. Louisiana residents add 4% sales tax ($0.64 per book purchased).

_____ Check if gift wrap is desired . *(Please add $1.50 per copy gift wrapped.)*

_____ Enclosed is my check or money order for $_____.
Make check payable to Sugarfree New Orleans.

_____ Charge to ___ VISA ____Mastercard ____AmEx

Card No._____

Exp. Date_____ Name on Card _____

Signature_____

Name_____

Address_____

City_____ State_____ ZIP_____

Telephone_____